HOMILIES ON THE "A" CYCLE OF READINGS
FOR SUNDAYS AND HOLY DAYS

Some men among them began to speak,
announcing the good news
of the Lord Jesus.
(Acts 11:20)

ANNOUNCING THE GOOD NEWS

HOMILIES ON THE "A" CYCLE OF READINGS
FOR SUNDAYS AND HOLY DAYS

alba house

A DIVISION OF THE SOCIETY OF ST. PAUL
STATEN ISLAND, NEW YORK 10314

CHARLES E. MILLER, C.M., OSCAR J. MILLER, C.M. and MICHAEL M. ROEBERT

Imprimi Potest
    Joseph S. Falanga, C.M.
    Vice Provincial, Los Angeles Vice Province

Nihil Obstat
    John A. Grindel, C.M.
    Censor Deputatus

Imprimatur
    Timothy Manning, Archbishop of Los Angeles
    July 19, 1971

Library of Congress Catalog Card Number: **74-169144**

ISBN: 0-8189-0215-9

Designed, printed and bound in the U.S.A. by the Pauline Fathers and Brothers of
the Society of St. Paul, 2187 Victory Blvd., Staten Island, N.Y. 10314 as part of their
communications apostolate.

CONTENTS

Introduction

The end of our preaching and our worship is that we might grow in love together with the Pope, our Bishop and all the Clergy. Then our blessed Lord will be ready to present us as an everlasting gift to His Heavenly Father.

Whatever helps us to grow in His love is worthy of our attention. In such a manner do we view this book. It has three worthy priests as its authors. It is a fitting companion to the other works from their pens.

We commend it to priest and preacher. May it stimulate the appropriate language and technique which will be a vehicle for the proclamation of the word of God and for the response to it in faith and love.

✠ Timothy Manning
Archbishop of Los Angeles

To the Preacher

Every evening millions of Americans sit down to watch the news on television. Most of these programs do not stop with telling and showing what has happened. They also make an effort to interpret the meaning of the day's events. A man like Walter Cronkite, backed up with on the spot pictures, reports the news, while a man like Eric Severeid attempts to show its significance and implication for the viewers.

As preachers we are called by God "to announce the good news of the Lord Jesus." Within the liturgy ours is a twofold function, not only to report or proclaim the good things that God has said and done but also to show their significance and implication for people today. We must make the people contemporaneous with the scriptural events (exegesis) and we must make the scriptural events contemporaneous with the people (hermeneutic). To put it another way, we must make the people aware of what God has said and done as recorded in the scriptures, and we must help them to see what God is still saying and doing today as the scriptures take on a living reality within the Mass. Such is the purpose of the homily. "Its character should be that of a proclamation of God's wonderful works in the history of salvation, the mystery of Christ, ever made present and active within us, especially in the celebration of the liturgy" (*Constitution on the Sacred Liturgy,* 35).

As people sit and watch the news on television, they may have little or no effective reaction. To the word of God, however, they must not be allowed to remain unresponsive. First is a liturgical response, "for in the liturgy God speaks to his people and Christ is still proclaiming his gospel, and the people reply to God both by song and prayer" (*Op. Cit.,* 33). The scriptural proclamation, especially as made "present and active within us," should be used to move the people to respond through either praise and thanksgiving, sorrow, or petition. The liturgy of the word should lead to the eucharistic liturgy, for "the two parts which, in a certain sense, go to make up the Mass, namely, the liturgy of the word and the eucharistic liturgy, are so closely connected with each other that they form but one single act of worship" (*Op. Cit.,* 56). The homily provides the link between word and eucharist.

Response to God's word must find its expression also in daily conduct. And so the second response is one in life, for "by means of the homily . . . the guiding principles of Christian life are expounded from the sacred text during the course of the liturgical year" (*Op. Cit.*, 52). As love of God is incomplete without love of neighbor, so worship is incomplete without Christian living.

This theory of the homily may appear formidable to the preacher, especially when he is asked "to cover it all" within seven to ten minutes. What is proposed here, however, is not a four point structure for a homily (exegesis, hermeneutic, response in liturgy, response in life). The four points should be viewed rather as elements that color preaching, and their use should be dictated by the nature of the scripture readings themselves. A hermeneutic is always necessary, but while some passages need a lot of exegesis, others need hardly any. At times the call to liturgical response can be left implicit as the response in life is emphasized, or vice versa. Moreover, a single homily can hardly be expected to produce full fruit, but if a preacher is aware of the four elements for which he is responsible as a homilist, then over a period of time he will lead his people to an understanding of the scriptures in themselves and as a living reality to which they are to respond both in liturgy and in life.

Obviously a preacher must be a student, if not a scholar, of the bible and the magisterium. He must know what the scriptures mean in the light of the Church's teaching. And he must be a man of prayer in personal union with God. His is a prophetic role, to proclaim not only "Thus *said* the Lord," but also "Thus *says* the Lord God." In his role as prophet the priest must listen in prayer to God speaking within him through the Spirit. He must also know his people in order to make the word of God touch their lives in a practical way. He must not only talk their language but must also speak within the context of their lives. And he has to be a liturgist, not a theorizer or rubrician, but truly one for whom "the liturgy is the summit toward which the activity of the Church is directed, as well as the font from which all her power flows" (*Op. Cit.,* 10).

The television reporter and commentator are aided by compelling images. With their manner of presentation we are frankly in competition for the attention of our people. Does this mean visual aids for preaching? In some circumstances it does, but visual aids are more than slides and films. We must make our words create images for people, and in the final analysis we will always need the concrete word for exact communication. We must preach like Jesus, with simplicity, directness, and vividness. We have become so familiar with the words of Jesus that we run the risk of overlooking the definite techniques he used. Jesus expressed the most profound truths, not in the abstractness of classroom jargon, but in the simplicity of plain words and in illustrations drawn from life. Success in preaching can be achieved not only by preaching what Jesus preached, but by imitating his style as well.

The homilies in this little book are not meant to be a substitute for your own creative work after you have studied and prayed over the day's scripture readings in the light of your people's needs. They are intended to give you one approach to the day's liturgy, and hopefully a spark or stimulus to your own thinking as you prepare your homily. At best the words in this book are nothing more than cold, black print on a page. Only you the preacher can make what is behind these human words come alive as real spiritual communication.

The office of preaching is your gift from God by which you are to utter his praises in the assembly of his people (Ps. 22:26) as you fulfill your duty of "announcing the good news of the Lord Jesus."

C.E.M.

By your gift will I utter praise
in the vast assembly

(Psalm 22:26)

Prepare Now, Celebrate Later

Think how many mixed feelings occur around this time of year. Even before the Thanksgiving turkey has had a chance to settle, the blaze and glitter of Christmas have already appeared in all the shopping centers. And you think to yourself: "Gads, I've barely paid off last Christmas' bills. . . . A whole month to go, and the advertizers have their grubby, little hands out for business. How depressing, how materialistic, how un-Christmas." But be careful you don't share your thoughts with any children around. They'll probably disagree. They've been holding back excitement as long as they can. The shopping centers are merely proclaiming what any child knows to be a fact: Christmas is coming. How many youngsters will be waking early to ask, "Is it Christmas yet?" Or at least shouting in their own way with St. Paul: "Night is far spent—it's the hour for us to rise from sleep."

Jewish Excitement

St. Paul knew what it was to be excited, even as an adult. It was in his blood. Jewish excitement about a Great Coming spanned some 2,000 years. Each great writer in the Old Testament added dazzling predictions. A royal leader. Wealth and influence over all peoples. The Prophet Isaiah became Spokesman for the New Age. The Day of the Lord meant that swords would be made into plowshares, spears into pruning hooks. A time for all to dwell in the Lord's house on the highest of mountains. Nations would come to the Lord in peace. These ideas are part of the joyful expectation which Advent is about. The Jews historically looked forward to the coming Day of the

1

Lord. And we today are looking forward to Christ entering our lives in the Christmas celebration.

Warning

But there's a damper to this excitement. Christ is *warning* us of his Second Coming. And it almost sounds like disaster. He will come, as we profess in the Creed, but at a time we least expect. Had Noah's neighbors been as open to the Lord as Noah, the author of this sacred story could have written a different ending: many arks were built and all were saved . . . because they had faith to prepare for the flood. The same disaster can hit two families today: flooding, fires, robbery. But if one of the families has a fire prevention system, or solid fencing, good locks, they'll be spared. None of us has to literally stay awake around the clock looking for disasters, but we have to be wise and awake about anticipation and preparation.

Solution: Be Prepared

And this seems to be the solution to Our Lord's warning: simply, be prepared. The Lord *is* coming: he is coming in the Christmas event on December 25th. He is coming to our lives in each Mass we celebrate, through his Word and sharing his Life as food. And, he is coming at the end of time. We automatically prepare for the joy of the Christmas event: cards are sent out, presents are bought; and eventually, the house is decorated.

But St. Paul suggests making some permanent Christmas preparation. Try putting on the Lord Jesus Christ. This means getting "spruced up" interiorly. Look for some of your dark spots: lack of patience, petty jealousy, selfishness. Use Advent to brighten things up. Try to be a better listener, a better smiler. Put down the newspaper or turn off the TV once in a while and just listen to your family. Discover more about

Christ by reading the Gospels. Five minutes a day between now and Christmas would make you and Christ better friends.

This Mass

And obviously, Christ himself is here during this Mass to help us prepare to receive him now, and at the end of our own time. Let our Mystery of Faith response after the Consecration be confident and strong: Christ *will* come again! Pray during the Our Father: Thy kingdom come, Lord: into my own life, my family's, into our world. What a Christmas we would have, if there were peace and unity on the earth.

We don't want to be robbed of our Christmas joy and excitement. The thief we have to watch for is dullness and apathy. During the next few weeks, when you go shopping and see the trees and tinsel, don't protest. Simply be reminded to invite Christ to come! All of us want to be prepared and excited for Christmas. Especially that Christmas that won't end: the Second Coming of Christ. Maybe by then we will be prepared—to go home to the Father for the Eternal Holidays.

M.M.R.

Revival

It seems safe enough to state that most Catholics would be very uncomfortable attending a typical Protestant revival meeting, even though our new liturgy has introduced prayers and songs out loud. There's something unsettling about phrases like "Repent! Accept a personal Savior! Be saved, you sinners!" They are just not found in our prayer vocabulary. Even less familiar would be a minister who ranted and raved, swinging his arms and calling us to come forward. It is suggested that Billy Graham's popularity is due, not to his revival techniques, but rather to his low-keyed manner of approach. A wild revivalist hasn't got much of a chance with traditional Christians.

John the Baptizer

Even John the Baptizer had a difficult time. In fact, he must have been repulsive to the traditional Jews. After all, what stable, respectable synagogue-goer in his right mind would tramp out to the desert to see some "kook." "Ugh . . . you get all muddy, sloshing around in the Jordan." And the least of John's fans would have been the Pharisees with their sophisticated smiles, their condescending nods. These men must have supplied most of the fuel for John's fire. "You brood of snakes, reform your lives. The reign of God is at hand."

Hard Hearted Us?

Yet the most difficult people John has to reach aren't the Pharisees. We are. We are just not ready to accept a revival preacher. After all, we are staid, traditional Catholics who

4

certainly aren't Pharisees or hardened sinners. And we definitely don't need to reform our lives. Most of us consider ourselves "good." Had we been Jewish in the time of Our Lord, we would probably have agreed with the verdict that Christ was an upstart and a madman. We would continue to go faithfully to the synagogue and turn our backs on this unorthodox preacher who dined with criminals and sinners.

But how long will we remain blind and deaf to John's invitation? Will we continue to be slightly hypocritical saying: "Nothing really wrong with me. I come to Mass each Sunday. Donate to the Church. Don't make me have to think whether I'm honest in business, my tax returns. Whether I really love the black man, or the white man. No matter if I'm number one in my life and no one else really counts. After all, who can tell the difference? I look like a good Catholic. I sound like one. And we're all entitled to our private opinions: you can't love everyone. Especially if they're lazy, or on welfare, or just plain dirty. You can't worry about everyone. And who is going to take care of me, if I don't. Sure, I like Christ. But I have other things to worry about. My business. My ballgames. And besides, you won't catch me being a loud-mouth Catholic. When the crowd starts talking about abortions or wife-swapping, I just smile and go along with things. Better not rock the boat." How many of us sound a little like this? Let's face it: John is right. Most of us do need *some* reforming. If Pope John XXIII convinced the world that the Church is ever in need of self-reforming, then we'd better listen to Prophet John the Baptizer. "Please reform your lives. The reign of God is at hand."

Core of John's Message

And the core of John's message is not to condemn us, but to draw more attention to this Jesus of Nazareth. He wants to be a helpful road sign. Yet he wants to fade out of the picture like the best man who steps back when the groom comes in, or the servant not worthy to carry the teacher's sandals, or the pale dawn that longs for the full sun. John is merely trying to prepare us to meet Christ. He is trying to get us to be honest about ourselves, to recognize that we are weak sinners who need help. John's call to repentance, appearing so severe and full of gloom, is a strong invitation to follow and accept the Lamb of God who takes away our sins. John isn't pointing at us in accusation as much as he is pointing out Christ: the Bringer of Wisdom, the Kind Judge who will bring harmony to all men and nature. Christ comes at Christmas as a Child to lead us. The wolf becomes guest of the lamb. The calf and the young lion browse together. And men become brothers to each other, blest sons of a loving Father. Christ *is* coming at Christmas. This is a happy event. But Christ is also coming at the end of time to judge us. If we're chaff or debris, then we'll be cleared away and tossed into the fire.

Our Choice

We have a choice: to take John seriously or not, to fit Christ into our thinking or not. We can let his wisdom blossom in our minds. We can have pity on the poor and the helpless. We can accept one another, as we forget ourselves for our family and work for harmony—not just artificial Christmas cheer, but lasting Christmas concern.

During our "revival meeting" here today, John will announce again: "This is the Lamb of God who takes away the sins of the world. Happy are those who are called to his supper." Let us simply admit we do need help to become better, and be happy because in spite of ourselves Christ does love us and does accept us. He invites us to come forward. "Lord, I am not worthy to receive you, but only say the word and I shall be healed."

M.M.R.

6

God Can Do It

They say that history tends to repeat itself. I suppose that is true mainly because human nature does not change. The first reading today tells us that our first parents were sinful. And when they sinned, they looked around for excuses—the old human foible of "passing the buck." Adam said, "Don't blame me; blame that woman you gave me." And Eve said, "Don't blame me; blame that snake in the grass."

Human Nature

We are not really much different from our first parents. It is just very hard to admit that we are weak, that we are imperfect, that we have faults. Even in little things we make excuses. If we knock over a glass and break it, we protest that it is the fault of someone who left it where they shouldn't have. If we run out of gas, we try to blame someone else for having forgotten to fill the tank. And when it comes to sin, the degree of our guilt is exceeded only by the imagination we use in finding excuses.

Honesty

All of us can use a great big dose of honesty in admitting that as human beings we are far from perfect. The problem is that we are engaged in a bitter struggle against evil. God warned that from the time of the first sin enmity would exist between the devil and the human race. Enmity means all out war to the end. We simply cannot afford to overestimate ourselves any more than we can afford to underestimate the devil. And making excuses, pretending that we are stronger and better than we are, is playing right into the devil's plans, as did Adam and Eve. He is more subtle and clever than we can ever be.

Mary, the Maidservant

If we had to fight this battle alone, we would simply have to give up in despair. But we need not fight alone, provided we stand before God in honest humility and say, "We can't do it alone; we need your help." God will help us, and with him on our side we cannot lose. That is one meaning of today's feast, the Immaculate Conception.

With Mary God showed how powerful he really is. Mary was just as human as we are. But she was humble. When the angel appeared to her, she didn't say, "Oh, I know I'm great. I will get God's work done for him." No, she humbly professed, "I am the maidservant of the Lord." A maidservant, she said,— one who completely depends on her master. And God brought his almighty power to bear on the person of Mary. Through his power she was conceived without sin and remained without sin throughout her whole life.

Hope

What God did for Mary should give us hope. God has the power. Will he use it for us? Will he be on our side? Yes, he will, for, as we heard in the second reading, God has chosen us to be his children. And God will not abandon his children. He will help us through the struggle with sin if we first admit we need his help by not making excuses and if we turn to him with confidence and trust. We must stand before God naked like Adam and Eve—naked without any clothing of excuses to try to cover over our human weakness. And we must say to him, "We need your help to overcome sin. We know you can do it because we have seen what you have done for Mary Immaculate."

C.E.M.

Patience and Trust

Writers throughout the ages like Vergil, Homer, Shakespeare, Hemingway, Steinbeck, and Tennessee Williams have felt that man and nature are closely related. Each reflects the other. Something wrong with man? Nature would show it. Today's ecologists feel the same way—that pollution is reflecting man's problems. Smoke replaces air; asphalt replaces ground; DDT replaces streams. We're losing touch with mother earth . . . and ourselves. Even the "under 30" generation (the flower children of the late 60's) are prophets of ecology and nature. They propose setting up community farms in rural areas of northern California, Idaho, and New Mexico, so more can become farmers, close to the earth. But it may be feared that most of us, along with this generation of prophets-turned-farmers, in spite of our interest, lack vital basic qualities: patience and trust.

Isaiah the Farmer

The prophet Isaiah is a good teacher. With his patience and trust, he was a noble prophet who was a farmer at heart. He was willing to wait and see what would come, what would grow. And he trusted it would be wonderful. He compared the age of the coming of the Messiah (700 years later) to the desert of Israel in bloom with abundant flowers. Even Isaiah's descendant, the apostle James, warned the Christians of his day to be like the farmer: patient for the final coming of Christ—trusting in a new earth, the fullness of the new age.

Our Problem

The problem for our society today is, first, most of us don't

9

want to be farmers, and second, we demand immediate results. We lack trust or belief that a new world has begun. Where is its beauty or harvest? We see such hate and disunity: assassinations, corrupt politicians, gross misuse of the gift of sex. All of this looks more like the desert than the blossoms.

Yet, we have Christ's word that a New Age has begun, and his promise that the full blossoming of this Age is coming. In fact, Christ himself can be seen as a farmer, a planter sowing the seed of life with his death, watering it with his own blood, then bringing forth this life from the ground in his Resurrection. The first signs of the new harvest were the blind recovering sight, the deaf hearing, dead men being raised from the grave, and the poor having the good news preached to them. This was the report sent to John to convince him that a New Age had begun.

And today, this is the report sent to us in the readings of this Mass, to convince us that Christ has come into this world, and still is coming. If we look carefully, we can see new growths. The early harvest today is the hope that springs from the Second Vatican Council, the renewed liturgy of the Mass, the beginning of churches growing together, and the increased concern for the poor, handicapped, and sick.

Advent: Still Time to Grow

This Advent ought to be a time for us to water ourselves like the winter rains with Christ, so Christ can grow deeper in us. The only obstacles to growing are spiritual pollution: being blind to the real presence of Christ, stumbling over him instead of accepting him, grumbling against one another, being prophets of gloom. So few around us even take time out to ask if Christ is "He who is to come" and are looking for other answers: good appearance, security, comfortable homes. Without Christ we can only become petty, jealous of others' successes, and deadened to real life. Fr. Teilhard de Chardin—a man of the earth—suggests in his writings that when we "grumble against one another," or sin in any way, we slow down not only ourselves, but the progress of the world in all areas, moving toward the completing of the Age begun by Christ.

Prepare for a Brand New Day

John the Baptizer prepared for the coming of Christ by seeking him, listening to him. It's still not too late to germinate the seed of Christ growing in us through our Baptism. Christ now waits to come to us in this Mass, if we seek him, listen to him. Ultimately he can lead us to full growth in his Final Coming. Be patient, my brothers; the Lord *is* coming. Be patient with the political world coming to its fullness in Christ. Be patient with your family and friends, learning to come to Christ. And be patient with yourself, your weakness. During these last two weeks before Christmas, prepare the way for Christ to come in: smile, listen, take others seriously. Who knows? Perhaps men all over will become more patient and trusting with each other—more capable of treating physical and spiritual pollution. Then nature will certainly reflect the new sunlight: the Light of God's Son shining on a brand new day, a Christmas Day without end.

M.M.R.

Spiritual Liberation

The early 70's may go down in history books as the high point in the emancipation of womanhood. The woman's liberation movement has propelled women into the political limelight. Commercials remind women of their newly discovered freedom in fashions and housekeeping. But what is heralded as a breakthrough in this century is only part of a long line of history.

Ahaz

It started ages ago—in fact some seven hundred years before the birth of Christ. The status of women indeed needed elevating, especially in Palestine. Politically and religiously it was truly a man's world. Even the hope for a Messiah, a great new leader, was founded on David's dream that one of the long line of male descendants would be the Messiah. So the thinking went until the day the prophet Isaiah was moved by God to confront Ahaz, the reigning monarch. Ahaz was a shrewd statesman. He had made alliances with all the great states surrounding Palestine. Each agreed to protect Palestine against the others' countries. Ahaz was proud of his shrewdness, and that is what disturbed Isaiah. Ahaz had given up any notion of needing God.

Promise

Isaiah came to ask Ahaz to put his trust in God and promised to give him a sign. Ahaz proudly refused to comply under the pretense of not wanting to tempt God. But Isaiah gave him a sign anyway, a sign of God's continued protection and guidance by promising that a young woman would bring forth a

Savior, and his name would be Emmanuel, "God-with-us." This passage as read by the Church and understood in the light of further and full revelation brings the figure of the woman, Mother of the Savior, into a gradually sharper focus. When looked at in this way, Mary is the virgin who is to conceive and bear a son, whose name will be Emmanuel.* So it was that Christ our Lord was to be born of the House of David, but through Mary's side of the family. And woman's road to dignity began.

Mary and Joseph

Yet even modern feminists will admit that women can't do everything alone. Not even Mary, the chosen mother of the Messiah, could do so. A holy and good man was chosen, a loving husband, Joseph. And Joseph was no dim-witted husband out of a kitchen cleanser commercial. To begin with, he didn't suddenly discover that Mary was pregnant. Mary was obviously in love with Joseph and would have confided the angelic revelation. Nor was Joseph afraid Mary would be punished for bearing a child out of wedlock, for Jewish law recognized engagement as a solemn binding contract and allowed the couple to live as husband and wife. What Joseph feared was his own unworthiness to act as father of a child who came from God, and he did not think himself holy enough to care for Mary since God had personally chosen her for a great task. The only answer he could see was to back out of the picture with a divorce. Then he was told to have no fear about taking Mary as his wife and he was instructed to accept the child by giving him his name, Jesus.

Good Balance

And a good balance began: a humble man caring for his young wife, and together in God's providence raising and offer-

*Cf. Vatican II's Dogmatic Constitution on the Church, 55.

ing to the world its Messiah. They were a man and a woman sharing a great responsibility. Mary and Joseph became an example to all of us, not dictating to God how they would like their lives to go, but accepting life's events as gifts for growing closer to God.

Yet Mary and Joseph are not unique. God the Father can work miracles in all of us by placing his Son in our minds and hearts. And he will do so if we offer ourselves to God as Mary and Joseph did. Christ can be born in us only if we lay aside basic human pride and admit we need help. This is why we are here at Mass: to receive the gift of Christ, to discover that someone really cares about us, not just during the Christmas season, but for the rest of our lives. And we assume our true dignity as Christian brothers and sisters, equal before God our Father. No need for a spiritual liberation movement. The Father frees us from the bondage of sin with his forgiveness at the beginning of Mass, and makes us worthy to stand around the altar with Christ his Son. Christ prepares himself and us to be a gift to the Father. What a fine preparation for Christmas: Christ and we become the gift and the givers, giving ourselves to the Father and each other.

Perhaps the decade of the 70's will go down in history as the awakening, the liberation of men and women to their highest dignity as mature Christians called by the Father to accept one another with equal worth, while anticipating our final glory in the second coming of Christ, the final liberation of all men and women to live as one with the Father.

M.M.R.

(The following two homilies can be used separately for Midnight Mass or Christmas Day. They can also be combined for a slightly longer homily.)

The Great Christmas Gift

For the last four weeks we have been like children expecting a large package in the mail. We've known it was coming. It was just a matter of waiting for the day. And tonight the Gift has arrived. And like children, even before the official presenting of the Gift, we've peeked inside. We know already the Gift is Jesus Christ sent to us from God our Father.

But even knowing that it is the Son of God arriving, we can't help but be stunned by the special way the Gift is wrapped. For the Father presents his Son wrapped in the clothes of a baby. What hardened person, what calloused Scrooge isn't moved by the sight of a newborn child? Instant welcome, instant love is felt for the child—a far cry from the rejection to be experienced by this child when he reaches his manhood.

And how amazing that during this birth celebration in which we receive the Eucharistic Bread, the Child should be born in a city whose name means House of Bread, Bethlehem. And more, he is laid in the manger, a symbol of nourishment. The Father suggests that he gives us the Son to become a part of us, to be our Food of life.

Great Exchange

And tonight we experience history's greatest exchange of gifts. Jesus Christ takes the gift of our humanity with all its vibrance and beauty, and gives to each of us in return a share in his divinity, making us his brothers. Our simple humanness takes on a glow. We are no longer creatures staring up at a giant creator. We become different—going from confused orphans of this world, to richly rewarded, adopted sons of a great Lord. Our destiny becomes clear. Our inheritance guarantees eternity for us: an eternity of knowing we are loved, wanted, accepted and treasured by God. After all, we are members of his family.

Sharing the Gift

And like a child showing a new gift, we ought to share our confidence and sense of hope with our brothers in this world who have no hope, no vision of the future. How good it is that many people choose Christmas as the one time of year to visit a Catholic service. During the greeting of peace, we ought to share not only the peace of Christ, but our confidence, our hope, our happiness which comes through Christ, our Gift. Again and again we could invite our neighbors and friends to attend Mass, to become close to the experience of God among men.

Complete the Cycle

And tonight, we have the opportunity to complete the giving cycle by offering anew the body and blood of Christ to the Father but with an added dimension. The Gift is not Christ alone, for we have become one with Christ. The Gift is not just the perfection of Christ but our added imperfections—our willing to try to be people of hope, proud possessors of a precious gift: Jesus Christ. Our one body in Church this night is made up of new friends, new faces, those not able to attend often, those who may be avoiding Christ. All of us join together in our weakness as children, happy to be here and thankful for the Father's Christmas Gift: Jesus Christ.

M.M.R.

16

The Ambassador

A century ago it was the custom of great nations to send their young sons to foreign countries to learn the customs and temperament of another people. Then when the youngster grew up, he would be in a unique position to understand both his own country and the land to which he had been sent. He would have the delicate role of negotiating treaties and trade agreements. And as remarkable as it would seem, he would be loved by both countries.

Jesus Christ Has Come

With all the beauty, warmth, and flourish that the Christmas season can provide, a great young Ambassador has come to our land. He has come to be like us in all aspects. In learning our qualities he will be able to share with us his background. He comes as the Son of a Great Ruler who wishes to establish ties of love, who places full trust and authority in his Son. God our Father has sent his Son Jesus Christ as a boy child to become a man like us in all things except sin. He is the greatest Christmas gift mankind has ever received: a Child who is God himself. How many thousands of generations have longed to look at the face of God. And in one simple gesture of birth, God shows himself to our time: a Father who loves, a Son who loves. That Son will love enough to offer up his precious human life on a hill in Palestine to bring the love of the Father to us. And the joyful, generous Father will seal this gift with the eternal promise of the resurrection, not only for his Son

17

who deserves it, but for all who believe in his Son, for all who call themselves brothers and sisters of Jesus Christ.

Eternal Christmas

Christmas is a passing day, and seldom are Christmas gifts long lasting. But today we receive the Gift of Life. As the coming of a child into a family is a beginning with the promise of growth, so the real Christmas is receiving Christ on a permanent basis, first as the Ambassador from the Father, and secondly as a Brother who cares. Christ comes as a Child to convince us that he will not hide behind his divinity in a kind of diplomatic immunity from human want, worry, and pain. He will go before us, experiencing the problems of life. Then he will turn back and suggest a way for us to travel.

Christmas for us is people: family, friends. But more, Christmas is a Person: Jesus Christ. He comes to show us how to live by loving; how to grow by suffering. In greeting others with Merry Christmas, we become envoys of Christ, spreading not just Christmas cheer, but extending his loving concern. Perhaps some day world powers may come to recognize our Ambassador Christ. Then truces can turn into lasting peace, and we can celebrate an Eternal Christmas.

M.M.R.

The Father's Family

Think how easy it was for Jesus to grow up as a perfect young man. He was raised by two saints: Mary and Joseph. Or to turn it around, Mary and Joseph found it easy to be saints as parents simply because Jesus Christ, Son of God, was their child. No problems. Except there were the poor living conditions at Bethlehem. And the time Jesus was "lost" in the temple—certainly a lack of communication there. Or Mary "forcing" her son into action at Cana, simply because he was unwilling to "show off." Or more seriously, the biting shame of having her son arrested as a criminal and the tragic loss when her son was executed. Every family has problems, even the best family.

Jewish Family

But the Holy Family is special. And sociologists today would suggest an additional reason why the Joseph of Nazareth Family is special: it's a Jewish family. In fact, of all the ethnic groups in the United States, Jewish families have the smallest number of juvenile delinquents. The style of Jewish family life may present a clue. Jewish children grow up experiencing their father as the representative of God in the family. Many Jewish feastdays are times of family celebration and the father presides over the prayers. He blesses the children as God's representative. Then growing up, the children can accuse their father of getting bald, not being the greatest ball player in the world, but they can never deny that he represents God.

Catholic Fathers

How many Catholic fathers lead their families in prayer,

19

or bless them before they go to bed? Without slighting a mother's role in the family, more fathers could recognize their God-given authority to be a family-teacher, a family-prayer-leader. Most fathers try year after year to provide the best of everything for their family. And they become "unknown" heroes since they are gone from the family for most of the day. But how impressive it would be for any family to have the father's presence be a joyful reminder of God, as Joseph reminded his family of the Father. All fathers aren't perfect, but each one reflects the loving care, the protection of our Father in heaven. Each father has a special patron in heaven, God the Father, and should make demands on the Father. And if more families could rely on the blessings flowing from the head of the family, perhaps less disunity and mistrust would be present.

Larger Family

Mothers and fathers try hard to make family life happy. But all families aren't bursting with joy. And some homes wind up being miserable places to live. Yet, ultimately all of us, whether we have a perfect family situation or not, can be happy in the bigger family we belong to. As St. Paul says: ". . . You are God's chosen ones, holy and beloved." All baptized Christians are adopted children of the Father. All the love that adopting parents bestow on their long-awaited children is ours. This love and concern from the Father should prod us as Paul suggests to have "beautiful mercy . . . kindness, humility, meekness, and patience" at home. We ought to "bear with one another, forgive whatever grievances you have against one another. Forgive as the Lord has forgiven you."

Father's Family

The Christmas season is very much a time for family celebration. It is sad when a person is alone at Christmas time.

So this Mass is a family celebration. Someone may meditate well alone on a mountain top, but when he wants to celebrate he comes together with others—as we are gathered here. And the sign of our familyhood is that we gather around our Father's table. As one family, we sing from our hearts in psalms, hymns, and other inspired songs. And the Father nourishes us with life-giving Food: his own Son. Mass by Mass our own sonship grows. Let us pray during this Mass for our own families, but especially for each other—that we may long for the day when all of us will finally be home with the Father.

M.M.R.

Happy New Life

Every mother knows the feeling of relief that comes after her child has been born. The several months of worry and concern as to whether her baby will be born healthy have made her anxious and tense. Finally the baby comes. Her anxiety turns to love and protection, as she cares for her child. A mother even possesses a special sound system whereby she recognizes her baby's voice during the night or in a crowd. A mother is preoccupied with her child.

Mary's Child

Today we celebrate the time when Mary was preoccupied with her child. First were the nine months of waiting and then the days of watching and listening for her child as she went about her normal duties as Joseph's wife, caring for his home. But always the delightful thought of Jesus was on her mind.

Clue

And all this can be a clue for our beginning the new year. Quite simply we need to be aware of Christ, or better, preoccupied with him in a special way. As we go about the normal activities of our lives we should have Jesus on our mind just as good parents have their children on their mind even as they go about their daily duties. Christ should take a position in our minds and hearts, not like the highway patrolman whom we fear as we drive, or the teacher whom the grammar school student watches out of the corner of his eye. Rather it should be as a child, or perhaps a friend, holds a corner of our mind. Jesus should occupy a part of us.

Place for Christ

We welcomed Christ at Christmas. He is here. He has come to be a friend, to join our family, to be a part of our existence. But what do we do with Christ? Is he to be like a picture of a relative who has passed away, a picture hanging on the wall and scarcely ever catching our attention? No, Christ is alive. He comes again in this Mass. He speaks to us in the scriptures. He greets us through the person next to us in the sign of peace. He gives us himself in communion. At the end of Mass do we smile a goodbye and leave him here in church, or does he go with us through the door?

No Burden

The beauty of Christ's presence is that he rides lightly on our minds. He is there for a moment's recollection, like remembering a good time we've had or a good friend we've been with. Uniquely Christ is not just a memory, for when we think of him, he is present and as real as he was with his mother and his disciples. The breakthrough was Mary's acceptance. By simply agreeing to be the mother of Christ she set aside her personal wishes and gained the world. How much more would we gain if we could only learn the art of gracious acceptance, to accept Christ as he is present here in the Mass, in ourselves and in others.

Seeing and accepting Christ, we could then learn to accept others as they are, not as miniature versions of ourselves, without making harsh demands on them. We should begin our year' by saying to ourselves, our family, our friends, our world: "The Lord bless you and keep you. The Lord let his face shine upon you and be gracious to you. The Lord look upon you kindly

23

and give you peace" (first reading). All this we can say since we will have Christ during every anguished moment of the coming year.

New Life

God our Father has struggled dearly to bring us to birth again in a new year. Each year gives us a fresh chance to grow in sonship with Christ, to call God our Father, to renew our adoption. How happy and relieved God will be when through death we are really born, really delivered home. Then it will be a happy new life.

M.M.R.

Follow that Star

Isn't it amazing in this age of science and sophistication that there is so much interest in horoscopes and astrological signs? It isn't long before most friends discover each other's birthdate and star sign. And all of us are secretly pleased when the newspaper prophet predicts a day to take life easy and be prepared for something grand to happen.

Ancient Man

With today's outlook, it isn't too hard to appreciate ancient man's dependence on stars and heavenly occurences. Any event in the skies caused excited expectation. The heavens were the television screen of the gods predicting in some hidden way man's coming events. It was natural for Matthew to choose the star as the sign of pagan men hoping for answers from heaven.

Whether it was a real or symbolic star isn't important. Matthew's narrative skillfully shows that Christ fulfilled the ancient predictions of the coming Great One. It also shows that nature responds more appropriately to God than man, that foreigners were more adept at recognizing Christ than the Jews, and that the mission of Christ was to extend to a world scene far beyond that of Palestine. And the wise astrologers were blessed. Of all who must have noticed a special star, they were the most eager. They yearned to join the new King.

Happy Longing

Longing for something is usually a delightful experience. We all experienced the longing for the warmth and surprises

25

of Christmas. And very often the longing, or expectation of something is happier than the actual event which comes and goes in a flash. Longing for a home of your own, or planning a vacation in the future can be a delight.

And on a deeper level, picture the husband and wife who long to get away from the kids just to be alone and appreciate each other. The second honeymoon might never come, but just longing for it is a good sign of the love that exists between husband and wife. It proves that love is there. How sad if that desire ever disappears.

And how many of us would long to get away from job and distraction, just to spend more time with our Lord. "I'd go on a retreat right now, if I could get away." "I'd love to spend more time in prayer at home, but the phone rings, the kids come in. I get so distracted, that Christ seems a million miles away." As disheartening as it seems sometimes, there is a good side. Be happy you have the desire to reach Christ. This desire, this longing only shows how limited things are on this earth. Only in heaven will we possess Christ perfectly. He'll be right there face to face.

You Are Not Alone

Some of the greatest saints in history, St. John of God, both St. Theresas, St. Francis of Assisi, all had to fight the problems of business and distractions. But the struggle of years never dampened their longing for Christ. And in the end, their patience with themselves and their life situation won Christ for them. Epiphany celebrates Christ showing himself to the world. But even Christ our Lord had to be patient to wait for thirty years before the right time came to fulfill what he longed for.

Be Patient

The longing of the wise men brought the reward of the discovery of the Christ child. Our own patience with our longing for Christ will give us Christ. Don't be impatient with your distractions in prayer or even at this Mass. Be happy about this desire you have. Know that Christ will come to us. He comes in this Mass to increase our faith, our hope to be closer, our imperfect love. And don't worry, you're not lost. If you long for Christ, you're following the right star.

M.M.R.

Here We Go Again

A promising young man is chosen and blessed by God to lead a new people. He walks into the Jordan for a ritual cleansing. He emerges and quickly chooses twelve men to be his assistants. Of course it sounds like Jesus Christ. But a thousand years before Christ a young man named Joshua emerged from the Jordan to lead the twelve tribes of Israel. He was a prefigurement of Christ. This helps to explain why the sinless Christ should seek the baptism of John. Christ walks into the Jordan to become the new Joshua, or better, the New Israel going through the waters of the Red Sea. As Christ comes out we have a New Exodus from the old incomplete Judaism to the freedom and potential of the New Israel, the Church.

Second Chance

So today we the Church celebrate a new beginning, probably a more realistic one than the New Year's Eve resolutions. For a week we've been able to rest from the holidays and settle down to routine. Now we can decide if this year is really going to be a different year for us. But it is hard to change, isn't it? The trouble is that so much of what we do is repetitious. We fall into a pattern of getting up, going to work, attending school, making beds, doing the dishes, and all of a sudden it's Christmas again. Another year slips right by us. But rather than look for some spectacular change, we ought to face the core of the problem head on: routine events, monotony, the drab rhythms that carry our days through the year.

28

Value in Routine

Psychologists tell us we need our daily routine, a certain familiar pattern of events. If we had to examine and choose each small detail of our day, we would soon become frayed neurotics with nervous twitches. Our routine, even with its monotony, is the soft familiar support which cushions us against the more disturbing events which need concentration and decisions.

But even granting all this doesn't help much to spare us from the dullness, the lack of color in routine. How many housewives can easily clamor: "We never do anything." How many husbands: "If I didn't have to work this weekend we could go somewhere." Yet this admittedly mild form of suffering has a value. All of us would like to say next year that during this year we became a better person, closer to Jesus Christ. So why not use the monotony, the dullness of each day to achieve this?

Our Baptism

The clue is our own baptism. Baptism is the joining force with Christ. We were baptized into the death and suffering of Christ and shared in his resurrection. We accepted a symbolic drowning, being buried under the water of baptism, in order to rise to a new life. If we could mentally join our daily dull suffering with that of Christ we could enjoy a new life with him even now.

Begin

Today we can easily make a realistic beginning. We can start by facing the routine which fills most of our time and thereby grow from it rather than try to run from it. We can accept the daily grind with a new intention, with a new purpose, and embrace this mild suffering in order to unite ourselves with Christ, the Suffering Servant. Our monotony is the link which

29

joins us with the Suffering Christ. A slight irritation or dullness can remind us each day of Christ. Christ didn't mind repeating an action already done before by Joshua. We will less and less begrudge repeating our day to day actions if we are in rhythm with the suffering of Christ. By joining the suffering of Christ we will eventually share in the glory of his resurrection.

This Mass

Even this Sunday celebration of Mass will become routine now until the special beauty of Holy Week and Easter. This very repetition is the journey forward step by step toward the Father. We climb a steep mountain by circling the same sides again and again, but each time on a higher level. Make today a beginning. Renew your baptismal promises within your heart. Ask Christ to accept the ounce of suffering from each day as an investment in your future. Listen especially at the moment of the consecration: "On the night before he suffered, he took bread. . . ." Ask Christ then to take your suffering and offer it with his own. And yearn for the final step: your death and the end of monotony when you will hear the words: "Welcome home; you are my beloved. My favor rests on you."

M.M.R.

The Prism

Less than a month ago we celebrated the magnificent event of the birth of Jesus Christ. In the fullness of time, God the Father sent his only Son to be our Savior. All of the previous history of the world centered on that moment, and in a certain sense time stopped, and we started counting time all over again from that great moment in history.

Preparations

God made long and elaborate preparations for the sending of his Son. That preparation was largely a series of selections of people who would lead to the coming of Christ. It was a narrowing down process. In Adam God had called the whole human race to be his chosen ones. After sin God set apart a man, Abraham, to be the father of his chosen people. Abraham was followed by Isaac, and he in turn was followed by Jacob, who had twelve sons, the progenitors of the twelve tribes of Israel. From among those twelve tribes, God selected one, the tribe of Juda, to be his specially favored people. From within that tribe he consecrated one family, the house of David, as the source of the savior. Finally God chose an offspring of David, Mary, as the person to give birth to Jesus. With the coming of Jesus, God's action began to broaden, for Jesus came to be the Savior not only of the Jews, but of the whole world.

Deutero-Isaiah

Even during the period of selection in the Old Testament era God was gradually making it clear that the savior would be

31

for all men. The first reading of this Mass was composed as the Jews were being freed from their captivity in Babylon. It indicates that they would be a source of salvation for the whole world: "I will make you a light to the nations, that my salvation may reach to the ends of the earth."

Testimony of John

When John the Baptist saw Jesus, as we read in today's gospel, he realized that he was the fulfillment of all of the centuries of preparation in the Old Testament. John proclaimed, "Look there! The Lamb of God who takes away the sin of the world!" Jesus was indeed the Lamb of God, but as such he was much more than the paschal lamb, whose blood saved the Israelites alone in Egypt. He was the Lamb whose blood would wipe away the sin of all people of all time. John was the last of the prophets of the Old Testament, and in one sense he was speaking in the person of all of the prophets before him when he said, "After me is to come a man who ranks ahead of me."

The Prism

Jesus is like a prism. All of the light of God's truth and grace through the history of the Old Testament narrowed down to focus on his person. That truth and grace pass through Jesus to be diffused now to everyone, for all people of every nation are called to be God's new chosen ones. As St. Paul in the second lesson wrote to his converts at Corinth, "You have been consecrated in Christ Jesus and called to be a holy people, as are all those who, wherever they may be, call on the name of our Lord Jesus Christ. . . ."

The People of God

We too have been consecrated in Jesus Christ. We have been

32

baptized with the Holy Spirit, the Gift of God, who has brought us the fullness of grace. By no means should we have to suffer any kind of "identity crisis." We are the new chosen people of God, his spiritual children. Coming after Christ as we do, we stand at a vantage point of time through God's favor. All of the centuries of preparation by God for the sending of the Savior, all that Christ did in his earthly ministry, have been diffused through Christ to us.

As we progress through the liturgical year we will hear recounted at Mass the wonderful works God did in the Old Testament. We will also witness Jesus going about proclaiming the good news of salvation. Then in Holy Week we will once more see him as the Lamb of God who shed his blood for our salvation. We will celebrate his resurrection in the hope that we too will share in that resurrection. Today our use of the fourth eucharistic prayer will give us a summary of all of these things.

Thanks and Glory

The preface will remind us once again that it is right that we should give thanks and praise to God for all that he has done for us. An attitude of thanks and praise should set the tone of our worship here at Mass throughout the entire year. We will have that attitude if we remember who we are as the new chosen people of God, the people who now enjoy the benefit of all that God has done in the history of salvation.

C.E.M.

33

No Factions

After Pope Pius XII died, his successor was a little known Cardinal by the name of Angelo Roncali. Almost everyone asked, "Who is he?" or "What will he be like?" Some even referred to him with a certain disdain as merely a "transitional pope." Soon, however, the human warmth, simplicity and good humor of Pope John XXIII won the favor of Catholics, those of other religions, and even those of no religion at all. Anecdotes about him appeared in the secular press; he was good copy.

Vicar of Christ

It was certainly a wonderful thing that Pope John had such an appealing human nature. That appeal made it a lot easier to respond to him, especially considering that many felt he had a "hard act to follow." The engaging virtues of Pope John are ones that every bishop and priest could do well to emulate, and yet the essential quality of Pope John was not his warmth, or his simplicity, or his good humor, but rather that he was the vicar of Jesus Christ. There is only one Savior, Jesus Christ, and he is the one to whom we owe complete devotion and attachment.

Christ through Others

In today's gospel we saw the Savior call Peter and Andrew, and James and John, so that they might become fishers of men. Jesus knew that in the plan of his Father he was to spend only a limited period of time on this earth. And part of that plan was that after Jesus had ascended into heaven other human beings like ourselves would continue his saving work in this world. Of course the human qualities of Jesus' ministers make a difference, but true faith will help us see through these qualities, whether good or bad, to the person of Jesus acting through his bishops and priests.

Problem at Corinth

Sometimes undesirable qualities in a bishop or priest can turn a person away from religion. Perhaps it is even worse when appealing characteristics attract people not to Christ but solely to the person of the bishop or priest himself. Such was the case at Corinth when St. Paul wrote the letter we heard in the second lesson today. Some people said that they belonged to Apollos. Apparently they were attracted by the fact that he was an eloquent speaker, well versed in the scriptures (cf. Ac 18:24). For different reasons others professed allegiance to Cephas, another name for Peter, and still others to Paul. Such human allegiances produced factions and dissensions among the Christians at Corinth. Paul indicated that quarrels and factions based on attachment to the ministers of Christ were as absurd as thinking that Christ himself had been divided into several parts.

Problem Today

Despite Paul's vehement denunciation of factions at Corinth, there is no doubt that human qualities do affect our religious reactions. For example, when the changes in the Mass were introduced, some people thought that Pope Paul had gone too far, that he had destroyed the grand and beautiful dignity of the old Latin Mass. They objected that they could not pray

35

at Mass any more because of all the noise people were making with their responses and hymns. Though they were not exactly attached to a person in the Church, they were attached to an old way of doing things which the supreme authority of the Church, acting in the name of Jesus Christ, had changed for good and solid reasons. Though they did not profess allegiance to Apollos or Cephas or Paul as did the Corinthians, they were tied to a mistaken notion of tradition instead of being loyal to Jesus Christ, guiding his Church in the world today.

Looking at the other side of the problem, some people refuse to participate in Mass unless it is accompanied by a certain musical setting and enhanced by an intense feeling of community and led by a celebrant who freely improvises in a highly personal fashion. Certainly the Mass should be meaningful in a contemporary atmosphere—and there is no excuse for a careless, sloppy, and impersonal celebration of Mass—but no one should be so attached even to legitimate attempts to make the Mass significant in our own day that he fails to see the value and worth of the Mass, no matter what its manner of celebration may be. The balanced Catholic saw a person like Pope John XXIII in his essential role, that is, as vicar of Jesus Christ. And in the same way we must appreciate the Mass in its essential quality as the celebration of Christ and his people in our communal worship of the Father.

It's Complicated

Of course this whole question of human qualities is complicated. We are not disembodied spirits without emotions and feelings. Personalities of priests and bishops as well as styles of celebrating the Mass do make a difference. In this whole problem, however, we should not put Jesus in the position of the fisherman who tried four varieties of bait with no success. In frustration he threw some coins into the stream and muttered,

"All right, go and buy yourselves something you do like." As St. Paul pointed out, Christ is the one who died for us as our savior, and it was in his name that we were baptized. To him alone must we be attached with an unshakeable allegiance.

C.E.M.

Upside Down is Right

When Thomas Jefferson wrote the Declaration of Independence he stated that "man has been endowed by the Creator with certain inalienable rights. . . ." He specified three of these rights. The first was the right to life. The second was the right to liberty. The third he listed, not simply as happiness, but as the *pursuit* of happiness.

Pursuit of Happiness

Everybody wants happiness, but it is the most elusive of all human pursuits. Perhaps one reason is that we do not all agree on what makes for happiness. Some say you have to be rich to be happy. Others agree with the idea behind the beer slogan, "Live with gusto; after all you only go around once in life." Some insist, "Look after number one; take care of yourself." Others protest, "I want to be free to do what I want, when I want, and the way I want." And of course there is the cliché, followed by not a few, "Eat, drink and be merry for tomorrow you die."

Upside Down

Jesus disagreed with all these ideas. In fact in his proclamation of the beatitudes read to you a few moments ago in the gospel Jesus took all these ideas and turned them upside down. He said to be happy is to be poor, to be sorrowing, to be lowly, to be merciful, to suffer persecution. That sounds crazy to most people. The precise meaning of each of the beatitudes is not easy to explain—scholars have written many long commentaries on them. This is no wonder because though the beatitudes do not exhaust all of Christian teaching they do capture much of the heart and spirit of Christianity. Perhaps today in thinking further about only the first of these beatitudes we can appreciate better what it means to be a Christian and in the process discover how the upside down ideas of Jesus lead to true happiness.

Poor in Spirit

What does it mean to be poor in spirit? Many Christians throughout the centuries since the day Jesus proclaimed this beatitude have found happiness in embracing voluntary poverty out of love for God, but the primary concern of Jesus was not with how much people do or do not have. Surely Jesus had no illusions that destitution and happiness go together. Actually Jesus urged his followers to help overcome the destitution of others. When Jesus used the word, "poor," he did so against a whole background of Old Testament theology. The poor of the Lord in the Old Testament, the *anawim,* were those people who did not rely on any worldly means to fight the battle of life. They did not trust in wealth, or military power, or political shrewdness. They depended completely on God to protect them and lead them successfully through life. They stood before God, helpless and defenseless, trusting in him and him alone. They were the humble and lowly spoken of in the first reading today. They took refuge in the Lord. They were the poor in spirit.

Realistic

Does all this sound unrealistic? Many would say that it does. After all, you can't look after number one or live with gusto if you don't depend on money. You can't be free to do whatever you want if you rely on God for help, because his help comes only to those who keep his commandments. And yet we have the word of Jesus that poverty of spirit is happiness.

39

That happiness begins even now, as we see in the serene peace of the saints, who lived according to the beatitudes. In another way the words of Jesus look forward to a happiness that is to come in heaven, but that is realism. Even those who live only to eat and drink know that tomorrow they die. And then what? Is the pursuit of happiness so ephemeral that it must end with death? Eat and drink today and die tomorrow—what a bleak, depressing outlook on life!

Dependence

Others protest that to be happy you have to be self-made and self-reliant, the old rugged individualism idea. That is why they say you have to look after number one. They judge religion to be a crutch, a means of strength for a weak personality, a form of psychological support. But again where does realism lie? The realistic, mature person faces the truth. If a man is crippled, he must use crutches. To look upon his crutches with disdain, or in a moment of supreme foolishness to throw them away with the protest that he can be independent of them, is the height of unrealism and stupidity. The truth is that we are the creatures of God, the Supreme Being. We depend on him for our existence as well as for all the means of survival both in this world and in the next. You may call religion a crutch, if you like, but you must also be prepared to recognize that as human beings we are spiritually cripples. That is a harsh way to put it, I admit. But I hope that it brings out the truth that to be realistic and mature, as well as psychologically healthy, we must admit our complete dependence on God.

The New Anawim

St. Paul in the second reading recalled how God chose from among the Corinthians the weak, the lowborn, the despised, and those who counted for nothing to be his people, the new

40

anawim. We must realize that we too are called to be the new *anawim,* the people who are poor in spirit. In this Mass we should stand before God, conscious of the fact that we are helpless and defenseless, and that we must put our whole reliance on him.

As far as many are concerned, the beatitudes are an upside down view of life. An upside down cake, when it comes out of the oven, looks very plain and unattractive. But when it is cut and served, the appetizing part is then on top. At present the beatitudes of Jesus may not appear attractive, but when he comes in judgment Jesus will show that beneath the surface appearance his teaching contains both truth and beauty, leading to lasting happiness.

C.E.M.

Sharing with Others

Some time ago a man moved to a small Southern town where he lived in a large house all alone. Little was known about him, but it was said that he had an extraordinary talent for playing the piano. In a short time an almost mystic legend grew up about his abilities in every form of music from the most intricate of classical compositions to the wildest of modern styles. There was one strange thing about the whole situation: he refused to play in the company of anyone. Despite the urging and sometimes the pleading of those who had come to know him, he consistently stuck to his refusal. One day a woman, perhaps playfully, challenged him by saying, "I don't believe all this I hear about how you can play the piano. Give me a demonstration." The man answered, "What you have heard about me is true. I used to play for others, but no more. Now I play only for myself." The woman asked, "But why play only for yourself?" After a moment of silence the man responded, "I learned music by myself. I practiced long hours by myself. Now I choose to entertain only myself."

Unrealistic and Selfish

Perhaps your first reaction is to say that this story is unrealistic. You are amazed that someone with such talent could be ignorant of the fact that he had actually done little by himself, that he needed a piano which someone else had invented and others had skillfully produced, that he needed music which someone else had composed and others had printed, and so on in a long list of persons upon whom he depended. Most impor-

42

tant of all he was dependent on God who had given him his musical talent to begin with. You may also think the story is unrealistic because you wonder how anyone could be so selfish; talent is given to us to be used. Then too you may be questioning how anyone could possibly impose upon himself what was obviously a deep unhappiness and loneliness. And yet the story is true. The story is so true that it is repeated in different ways by many people, perhaps even by ourselves.

Today's Gospel

Are we really generous in the use of our God-given talents? Today in the gospel Jesus tells us, "Your light must shine before men so that they may see goodness in your acts and give praise to your heavenly Father." That is saying a lot. To begin with we must be honest about admitting that God has given us gifts and talents, in fact, everything that we have. We will profess this fact at the beginning of today's Eucharistic Prayer when we pray, "All life, all holiness comes from you," and we conclude the Prayer with the same sentiment by saying, "We hope to enjoy forever the vision of your glory, through Christ our Lord, from whom all good things come."

Once we recognize God as the source of all that we have, we must then realize that our gifts are to be used for the benefit of others so that they may see God's goodness in us. Today's first lesson gave us a few practical suggestions about sharing what we have with others: to feed the hungry and to give clothing and shelter for those in need. It goes without saying that we hear a lot of appeals both in church and outside church, but maybe we dismiss these appeals too readily. Perhaps we feel, as did the man in the story I told, that we have worked hard for what we have and now we deserve to enjoy it all ourselves. But that attitude is a contradiction of the truth that all we have comes from God, including the abilities we use in earning money as well as the energy we expend.

43

Sharing

Money, however, is not the only thing we should be willing to share with others. There are things which cost more than money, such as our time and our convenience. For some people writing a check for a charitable cause or dropping an extra dollar in the collection on Sunday is the easiest thing they can do, and that they are willing to do. But it may well be that someone you know needs, not your money, but a willing ear to listen to his sorrows and trouble. You parents may after a hard day be settling down to relax and watch TV when one of your kids comes in, bursting at the seams, to tell you about what happened in school. Or you kids, perhaps there is someone in your class that nobody seems to like, someone who never gets any attention. In all these and like circumstances we must be willing to share our time and our kindness with others.

Attitude

What is really needed, what Jesus is talking about in today's gospel, is an attitude of mind, a realization that God has given us all that we have, our abilities and even our personalities. God does not want us to hide our talents selfishly or to hoard our goods. He wants us to share what we have and what we are with others so that seeing his goodness in us they may learn to praise God, the source of all goodness.

C.E.M.

More Than Just Getting By

When you go to a doctor, you want to have the assurance that the man is medically well educated, that he has kept up on recent developments, that he is competent and experienced. You want a doctor who is conscientious, not one who will be satisfied with doing the bare minimum for you just so that he won't become involved in a malpractice suit. You rightly feel that your health is too important to entrust it to a charlatan, a quack.

Spiritual Well-Being

Your spiritual well-being is much more important than your physical health. What is at stake is not good health which at best can last only seventy years or so for most people, but eternal happiness and the fulfillment of the whole purpose of human existence. From time to time we all need a good spiritual check-up, a thorough examination. In one sense we are our own spiritual physicians, because under God we ourselves determine what our spiritual health will be. Maybe we are not spiritually well educated. More importantly perhaps we have not kept up on recent developments in the Church's thinking. As a result we may even be spiritual charlatans, spiritual quacks.

Avoiding Serious Sin

Let me explain what I mean. We have all learned somewhere along the line that to commit a serious sin, three things are required: grave matter, sufficient reflection, and full consent of the will. If one of the three conditions is not met, then there is no serious sin. But if we are only concerned with avoiding sin, especially by means of a strictly legalistic approach of looking for loopholes, then we are like the doctor who does the bare minimum so that he won't become involved in a malpractice suit. Our lives then are based on fear lest we find ourselves accused of a capital crime in God's court of law. Just getting by within the law is not what Jesus had in mind for the Christian.

The Spirit of the Law

Today's gospel is part of our Lord's Sermon on the Mount. In that sermon Jesus set forth, among other things, basic principles of Christian conduct. He said that he had not come to abolish the law found in the Old Testament. That law was an expression of God's will for his people, but because it was necessarily put in human words it was an imperfect expression of God's will. Jesus wanted to show that it was the spirit behind the law that really counts, and that spirit is found in a responsible, generous love of God and our fellow human beings. Jesus fulfilled the law first by his more complete teaching on love, some instances of which you have heard in today's gospel, and secondly by his own supreme example of love. Jesus did not ask his Father, "What is the very least that I must do in order to save the world, what is the bare minimum needed to get by?" No, Jesus responsibly and generously went all the way, even to death on a cross.

Recent Developments

The Church wants us to follow the spirit of the law as we see it in the person of Jesus. As the Church tries to guide us in this spirit, some people have become disturbed. They think the authorities have gone soft. Here is one example: it used to be that the Church forbade the eating of meat on Friday under pain of serious sin. We know that law has been changed, but does it mean that the Church believes that things should be

46

easier for us? Not at all. The whole idea behind the old law was to make us aware of the need to do penance for our sins and to offer a specific means for practicing that penance. It was a way of telling God that because we loved him we were sorry for our sins. And yet as a matter of fact some people were just keeping the letter of the law to avoid serious sin. They were not eating meat, it is true, but they were dining on delicious lobster or other meatless delicacies. The whole spirit behind the law of Friday abstinence was forgotten. Now the Church says to us: Do more than just avoid sin. The Church challenges us as adults to adopt our own means of penance. Today is a good time to examine yourself on what you have done for penance since the law of Friday abstinence was changed.

The Mass

We also know that we must go to Mass on Sunday. But there is a spirit involved in this law too. Jesus says that if our brother has anything against us, we should leave our gift at the altar and first go and be reconciled with our brother. In other words we must celebrate the Mass as responsible, generous people. Our worship of God our Father is pleasing to him only if it overflows into love for all his children. To tell God in the Mass that we love him while we despise or even ignore him in his children is a contradiction and certainly not the spirit of the law. Going to Mass on Sunday only to avoid sin won't do.

More Than Just Getting By

Jesus tells us today that just getting by is not enough. We certainly are not satisfied with a doctor who does the bare minimum for us, and we certainly should not be satisfied with doing the bare minimum in order to avoid serious sin.

C.E.M.

47

Staying on the Road

A pessimist can have a field day with the news, whether on TV or in the papers: war, riots, murder, hatred, catastrophes. What is wrong with the world? How did it ever get into such a mess? Can a loving God be charged with all this evil? That is a question which has troubled people of every age.

In the Beginning

God revealed to his chosen people that he made all things good in the beginning. Human beings were his special creatures to whom he entrusted all the rest of creation. That is what is meant by the opening verses of today's first reading. Also in the beginning the relationship between God and man was a wonderful thing. The Bible pictures God and man conversing, as they walked together in the cool of the garden. God communicated his interest in man, his care, his concern, his love. God loved man so much that he gave him a gift which none of the other living beings on this earth enjoyed, the gift of freedom. God desired a voluntary love from man because he wanted him to be his familiar, his friend, his child. But freedom is a two-way street: man could use freedom to get to God or to get away from God. Unfortunately the first man went in the wrong direction, and the human race by and large has continued to make the same mistake. Sin is the root of evil in the world, and the consequences of sin are evident today in our homes, on our streets, across the nation, around the globe. How necessary is the prayer of the responsorial psalm: "Be merciful, O Lord, for we have sinned."

Mercy

In the second reading St. Paul proclaims that God has been merciful to us. The first man's sin disrupted the relationship with God, but the second man's (Christ's) obedience gives the opportunity of reconciliation. "Just as through one man's disobedience all became sinners, so through one man's obedience all shall become just."

The gospel goes on to give evidence of Christ's obedience. The devil was up to his old tricks again. He tried to get Jesus to abuse his freedom by turning away from God to travel the road of selfishness and greed. But Jesus responded to the devil's temptations with loving obedience to his Father's will. The gospel episode represented a turning point in the history of mankind. In the desert Jesus reached a decision which set him on the road to the cross, the sacrifice of reconciliation which we celebrate in the Mass.

Communication

Lent reminds us that we must follow the road to the cross. The cross, however, is not the end of the road. Rather it opens up for us a whole new road, a freeway, that leads to resurrection with Christ. It is the only road that can lead us to peace and happiness. To stay on the right road we must keep in contact with God. We must pray. Jesus has opened the lines of communication for us. Because of him our prayers get through to God, as we beg for light and guidance on our journey. And God responds to us if we only listen. And listen we must, for Jesus warns, "Not on bread alone is man to live but on every utterance that comes from the mouth of God."

The Mass

The Mass is beyond doubt our best means of communicating

with God. Together as his children we talk to him in the Mass of our needs, our love for him, our sorrow for our failures. And God tells us his wishes and gives us his guidance through the words of scripture. But is Sunday Mass enough? The preface today reminds us that during Lent we are to be "more fervent in prayer." One way to be more fervent is to make the effort to get to Mass during the weekdays of Lent. Maybe every day is not possible, but can't you be here two or three times a week? Even once during the week would be good. You will find the word of God in the weekday readings a real source of strength and guidance, and you will be offered the extra opportunity of praying to God.

Private Prayer

To be more fervent in prayer also means carrying the spirit of the Mass into all the aspects of our lives. Morning and evening prayers, grace at meals, and especially just trying to be mindful of God at different times, all these things should be an important part of our day. And as we try to make decisions, or when we know we will be faced with temptations or problems that try our patience or our charity, we should turn to God and ask, "What do you want me to do? Show me the way. Help me."

On the Road

What a wonderful gift God has given us in freedom. But with freedom comes the possibility of sin, and sin alone can get us going in the wrong direction on the road of life. Prayer is what we need, communication between God and ourselves, in order to stay in the right direction on the road that will lead, not only to the cross, but to the glory and happiness of resurrection with Jesus.

O.J.M.
C.E.M.

50

God Reaching Out to Us

An elderly grandmother had prayed first thing in the morning ever since she was a little girl. But recently she has been reading the newspaper first. When asked if prayer had become less important to her, she replied, "Oh, no, I'm just looking to see what I should pray about." She certainly understood the value and necessity of prayer. Last Sunday we observed that during Lent we should be "more fervent in prayer." Prayer is a dialogue between God and ourselves. The highest form of this dialogue is our Mass, especially when we all gather together, as we are right now.

First Step

The first step in prayer is made by God. We've always begun our prayers, "In the name of the Father, and of the Son, and of the Holy Spirit." God reaches out to us where we are and in some fashion communicates with us.

The first reading in today's mass is a good example. Man had sinned, a horrible response to God's love. God's reaction was one, not only of justice, but also of mercy. He promised a redeemer, one who could restore the lines of communication between God and man. At one point in man's history God reached down into the desert country of Haran and touched the life of a man named Abram. And in touching Abram's life, he touched the lives of all of us. In the spirit of Christ we are all children of Abram, later called Abraham, for we are the heirs of God's merciful forgiveness. In the words of the first reading: "All the communities of the earth shall find blessing in you."

51

In the second reading, Paul in his letter to Timothy, repeats the same idea. "God has robbed death of its power and has brought life and immortality into clear light through the gospel." This thought is God reaching into our lives. Through St. Paul he is communicating to us his mercy and love. Did we realize this sufficiently when we responded a few minutes ago: "Lord, let your mercy be upon us, as we place our trust in you"?

God Touching Us

The fact that we have prayed, have even wanted to pray, is a sure sign that God has already touched us. A prayerful man named John R. Coburn has written well of God touching us in our lives (*Prayer and Personal Religion.* The Westminster Press. Philadelphia, 1957).

"Have you ever, for example, had the experience of standing outdoors at night alone, looking up into the heavens? As you look at this canopy above you, you are suddenly overwhelmed by a sense of the immensity and greatness and mysterious order in the universe, and with a sense of your own tiny insignificance in contrast. If you have ever had such an experience, both exalting and humbling you at the same time, God may have touched you, for this is one of the ways God breaks in on people.

"Many have been struck by their inability to direct their lives according to their own best intentions. They find themselves caught in patterns of behavior they had firmly resolved to avoid. Yet they have a vague, uneasy sense that something else or someone else is around, and trying to communicate with them. This is God breaking into their lives.

"If you have ever had the suspicion that the only problem you really have is yourself, then you may have an undercurrent in your life of feeling guilty . . . a persistent, gnawing, uneasy feeling. This is sometimes an opening into your life that God is responsible for, through which you can turn to him.

52

"You may have been taken quite out of yourself at one time or another. Men and women are inspired to become more than they normally are when they come face to face with saints. At these times you may have been touched by God."

The Mass

God is reaching out to us today, here in this Mass. We have been listening to his Son coming to us in the readings and homily. At our Sunday Mass we are like Peter, James, and John going up the mountain with Christ. According to the gospel account of today's Mass God communicated something to these three men that they would later communicate in God's name to the Church. This message is well summarized in the second reading of today. "God has saved us and has called us to a holy life, not because of any merit of ours but according to his own design—the grace held out to us in Christ Jesus before the world began but now made manifest through the appearance of our Savior." God the Father is communicating to us in sight and sound just as he did to the three apostles on the mount of Transfiguration. "This is my beloved Son on whom my favor rests. Listen to him."

The Creed

Each Sunday we respond to God's message by rising after the homily and praying together our profession of faith, the Creed. Maybe we ought to manifest a little more of the enthusiasm of Peter, "Lord, how good it is for us to be here!" Peter spoke out of his misunderstanding of the nature of God's kingdom, not realizing that Christ's kingdom is not of this world. But there was nothing wrong with Peter's belief in Christ. "You are the Christ, the Son of the living God," he had affirmed. So Christ did not rebuke Peter for his ignorant response to what he was seeing. His knowledge of the Old Testament

53

writings should have given him some indication of what Moses and Elijah were talking with Christ about. The Messiah was to do the will of his heavenly Father, even if it cost him his life. In showing them his beloved Son, God, our Father, was hoping to have Peter, James and John realize who and what this Son truly is, the Savior of the world. He would bring salvation to all through his passion and death. But it would all end in the glory of the resurrection. Peter's response to God reaching into his life was wrong on this and other occasions, but on Pentecost day he realized what it was all about.

God is reaching into our lives within this hour. He has been waiting for us on this Sunday, as he does on every Sunday, to communicate to us his love. This is what the Mass is: God reaching out to us in love and we responding in the sacrificial act of Christ. This is prayer at its highest level. Yes, Lord, it is good for us to be here.

O.J.M.

God Pours Out His Spirit

Lake Erie is dead, and Lake Michigan nearly so. This is the estimate of conservationists and ecologists. One has reached the point where it no longer supports life, while the other just barely so. Sometimes the clutter and wastes of human existence deaden, or nearly so, the Spirit, that is, the life of God in us. It is then that we need to pray, especially to say our best prayer, the Mass. That is why last Sunday we repeated a couple of times with Peter: "Lord, how good it is for us to be here."

Living Water

For a people living in a desert land where good water was scarce, living water, such as that found in Jacob's well, was a blessing. The living water, what we would call "fresh water," that bubbled from the rock after Moses struck it, revived a people dying of thirst in the desert. Traditionally both the rock of water in the desert and Jacob's well have been symbols of God showing his mercy to us in the Mass. It is here Christ gives us his life that we may have life. "It is rare that anyone should lay down his life for a just man, though it is barely possible that for a good man someone may have the courage to die. It is precisely in this that God proves his love for us: that while we were still sinners, Christ died for us." "This is my body which will be given up for you. . . . This is the cup of my blood, the blood of the new and everlasting covenant. It will be shed for you and for all men so that sins may be forgiven."

Our Sunday Mass should be a time of refreshment and rejuvenation for us. Like the woman in the gospel coming to

55

Jacob's well for good, refreshing, life-sustaining water, we should come to Sunday Mass with the same eagerness. Then, perhaps, we could leave Mass renewed in faith that here God has once more reached into our lives. From this living water of the Body and Blood of Christ we should have the energy and enthusiasm to tell all whom we meet: "This is the One you are looking for. He is the Savior of the world." We leave Mass like people into whom "the love of God has been poured out through the Holy Spirit who has been given to us."

Response

Jesus did not argue with the woman. He simply tried to make her realize the facts of the situation. He is God's gift to men, not in the silly way in which we use those words sometimes, but in the reality of the Incarnation. Perhaps God is saying to us right now: "If only you recognized God's gift. . . ." Certainly the woman was interested in life-giving water. But where was anyone to find a beautiful flowing clear stream in that desert? Jesus disregarded that objection, for he was talking about himself as the giver of eternal life. ". . . the water I will give shall become a fountain within him, leaping up to provide eternal life." Then the woman uttered her first prayer, and even though it was a selfish one ("Give me this water, sir, so that I won't grow thirsty and have to keep coming back here to draw water"), a "gimme" prayer, nevertheless God accepted it. It was a response to his communication, and consequently an acceptable prayer. From that first response Christ was able to lead the woman to an acceptance of him as Messiah. From that first response the woman became the instrument of many others believing in Christ.

In the words of this Mass we repeat the promise of Christ. "I have come that you may have life, and have it more abundantly" (Jn 10:10). In this Mass Christ asks us to believe: ". . . the man who feeds on this bread shall live forever" (Jn

6:58). How fervent is our prayer of "Amen" to God breaking into our lives with the words of holy communion: "The Body of Christ"?

Worshippers

We here at this Mass, and those at Masses all over the world, are those of whom Christ prophesied: "Yet an hour is coming, and is already here, when authentic worshippers will worship the Father in Spirit and truth." The Spirit of God does break into our lives with his truth. Let us not be like a rock which does not yield to God's gentle urgings, or even to the heavy striking of his word. "If today you hear his voice, harden not your hearts." "Come, let us sing joyfully to the Lord; let us greet him with thanksgiving. . . . For he is our God, and we are the people he shepherds."

Enthusiasm

But our Mass, like our other prayers, seems to lack enthusiasm and vigor. If we come here simply out of a sense of duty and obligation, time will hang heavy on us. Everything will seem too long, too different, too mixed-up. We need to realize, by telling ourselves over and over again, who it is that is communicating with us through the Mass. Even though we may not like the format, nevertheless God can and does speak to us while we are here. It is necessary that we take to heart the admonition contained in the response we prayed after the first reading: "If today you hear his voice, harden not your hearts." How much better off we would be, if we made our response to God communicating with us with attention and deep meaning. "Come, let us bow down in worship; let us kneel before the Lord who made us. For he is our God, and we are the people he shepherds, the flock he guides."

The woman in today's gospel, selfish as she was, was

57

intrigued with this man, a Jew, asking her, a Samaritan, and a woman, for a drink. She saw him there, but she had no idea of any conversation with him. But Jesus spoke to her, a good example of how God takes the first step with us. The woman's first reaction to Jesus' request for a drink was a protest. Our protests to God breaking in on our lives are numerous and widely different. God broke into our life in baptism, but most of us were too small to know what was going on. He broke into our lives again at our first holy communion, when we responded with childish wonderment, glee and assurance. The meeting of eyes with the one who is the love of your life was God again breaking into your life. Has your stability of response been better than the woman's in the gospel? Sometimes God enters into our lives through a tragic accident, or a sudden illness. Is our response to this communication a prayer, or a cry of "Why has God done this to me?" which in itself could really be a prayer of anguish? Response to God communicating with us: this is important, for this is prayer.

O.J.M.

Wash and See

Traditionally Lent has been a time of concentrating on the sacrament of baptism. Today's scripture readings are filled with allusions to this sacrament because the Church wants us to give close attention to the meaning of our baptism.

The Gospel

As far as we know the blind man in the gospel was not complaining about his plight. Nor is the man depicted by St. John as crying out after Christ for a cure. Born blind, he really had no way of knowing what he was deprived of. It was Jesus who took the initiative. Notice the little ceremony Jesus went through to cure the man. He made clay of spittle and dust and anointed the man's eyes. It is significant that St. John used the word "anointed" here. John probably chose it as an allusion to the rites of baptism. The earliest Christian writers recognized that the evangelist intended his readers to see the realization of Jesus' sign in the sacrament of baptism. Jesus also made the point that the man received his sight only after he had fulfilled the command to wash in the pool of Siloam, a washing which also makes us think of baptism.

In our own sacrament of baptism Jesus took the initiative by giving us the call to become Catholics. For most this call came as infants, for others as adults. In either case it was "as Jesus walked along, he saw a man who had been blind from birth." He knew that we had been born blind spiritually, and he broke into our lives with the sacrament of baptism.

Spirit and Light

The other readings today also have something to do with baptism. The first speaks of an anointing and its result. God sent Samuel, the Judge, to Jesse of Bethlehem. From among the sons of this man, Samuel was to pick Saul's successor as king. Seven sons were brought before Samuel, but he rejected them all. When he found out that there was still one son, the youngest who was tending sheep, he asked that he be sent for. As soon as Samuel saw this young man, whose name was David, he knew he was the one. "Then Samuel, with the horn of oil in hand, anointed him in the midst of his brothers; and from that day on, the spirit of the Lord rushed upon David." Samuel went through a ceremony of anointing not unlike that in baptism. The priest anointed us with the sacred oil, and truly the spirit of God rushed upon us.

In the second reading St. Paul spoke of the Christian as one coming out of darkness into light, as one born blind gaining the power to see. His words should make us think of the candle the parents and godparents hold for the infant in the ceremony of baptism, as the priest says, "Receive the light of Christ."

Response

In the gospel story there are two reactions to what Jesus did, that of the Pharisees and that of the man born blind. The Pharisees were people who refused to see. At first they would not accept the fact that the man before them had been born blind. His parents had to be dragged into court to prove that he was their son, that he had been born blind, and that he had been cured. Despite all the evidence, the Pharisees did not want to admit the cure because they did not want to have to believe in Jesus. Jesus tried to enter their lives, but they would have none of him. They preferred to remain spiritually blind. When the man told his judges and accusers that Jesus was from God, their response was typical of those who do not have the humility to accept Christ: "You are steeped in sin from your birth, and you are giving us lectures?" They threw the man out and in the process threw out Christ as well.

The man who had been cured did not make the mistake of the Pharisees. When Jesus sought him out and asked for a profession of faith, the man responded: "I do believe, Lord." His meeting with Christ had brought him not only physical sight but spiritual vision as well.

Renewal

Faith was God's gift to us in baptism. We were led from darkness into spiritual light. At the conclusion of Lent we will be asked to renew our baptismal vows, but we really do not have to wait until then. We can make that renewal right now. As we stand for the profession of faith, the words should come not only from our lips but also from our hearts. Our "Amen" as a response to the words, "The Body of Christ," at communion should mean "I do believe, Lord." And when we leave Church we should do so with faith that Jesus is our Good Shepherd, as we professed in the responsorial psalm. He will satisfy our needs. We need fear no evil because he is with us. Through all the dark valleys of life he will lead us along the right paths to the house of his Father where we will live forever. How fortunate we were that as Jesus walked along he saw us and stopped to cure us of spiritual blindness. What a blessing it is that we can see Jesus with the light of faith and say, "I do believe, Lord."

O.J.M.

Hope -- For Now

We are not sure what kind of person Lazarus was. We may feel that since he was a friend of Jesus he must have been a good man, but we must remember that Jesus associated with all kinds of people, including some notorious sinners. Actually the point of importance to us is not that Lazarus was good or bad, but that he was dead and was brought back to life. Lazarus received the effect of God's great love, which we hope to receive too.

God does not wait until we are worthy of his love. Jesus himself said, "I was sent not to call the just, but sinners, to repentance." And just two weeks ago at Mass we heard St. Paul telling us: "At the appointed time, when we were still powerless, Christ died for us godless men. It is rare that anyone should lay down his life for a just man, though it is barely possible that for a good man someone may have the courage to die. It is precisely in this that God proves his love for us: that while we were still sinners, Christ died for us."

Baptism

Lazarus' condition in the tomb resembles ours before baptism, and his resurrection is like our reception of baptism. A dead person can do nothing for himself. We were like dead persons, but God took the initiative and gave us spiritual life through baptism. The second reading of this Mass told us: "If anyone does not have the Spirit of Christ, he does not belong to Christ. But . . . you are in the spirit (that is, not dead, but alive), since the Spirit of God dwells in you."

Actually it might be a valuable question to ask, "What kind

of person was Lazarus after his resurrection?" He was a living witness to the prophesy of the first reading in today's Mass: "Then you shall know that I am the Lord, when I open your graves and have you rise from them"—and that is why the enemies of Jesus tried to kill Lazarus. What kind of life would you lead, if you had been dead and brought back to life? Certainly you would go around telling everyone you met all about it. You would express, in your own words, the sentiment of today's responsorial psalm: "With the Lord there is mercy, and fullness of redemption." How great would be your trust in God! It would be so great that you would not fear even enemies who wanted to kill you.

Hope

We were in a real sense dead before baptism, spiritually dead. God took the initiative and broke into our tomb to bring us to life, spiritual life. How great should be our trust in God, with fear of no one. Baptism gives us hope. Let me tell you about a woman who knew what real hope is, Carson McCullers, the American novelist. At the time of her death Mrs. McCullers' career was described by a literary critic as a "vocation of pain." Before she was twenty-nine she had suffered three strokes which paralyzed her left side. She was so discouraged that she thought she could never work again. But gradually, a page a day, she resumed her writing, despite her pain. Then her husband committed suicide. In a rare mention of her troubles she said, "Sometimes I think God got me mixed up with Job. But Job never cursed God and neither do I. I carry on."*

Challenge

"I carry on." That is a response of real hope and trust. Maybe we are using alcohol, drugs, sexual freedom, excessive

*Christopher Notes, no. 170.

63

pleasure, disregard for the rights of others, maybe we are using all these things or more, simply because we are not responding to God in hope. All evils in the world today are not necessarily God's punishment. Rather they can be looked upon as a challenge to us to put our trust in God and then go forward with positive and constructive measures of reform and improvement. Hope does not mean only a response to God concerning the next world. It just as surely also means a response to God for now.

Now

Think about the conversation between Jesus and Martha in today's gospel. When Jesus said that Lazarus would rise again, she responded: "I know he will rise again in the resurrection on the last day." Martha found no difficulty in hoping for God's mercy at the end of the world. What she had trouble with was the now. Maybe we are the same.

God has broken into our lives a sufficient number of times to prove that he loves us. Why are there not better proofs of our response in hope and trust? Why do we not have more confidence in our prayers, especially when we pray together as we are doing right now? We pray for mercy many times in the Mass. Why can we not trust God to grant us his forgiveness now? We pray for peace. Do we trust God to answer our prayer this year? Our gathering together in the name of Jesus should itself be a confident prayer that will give us the power to put our hope into action *now*. Let's remember the word of God in the first lesson: "I have promised, and I will do it." And that means not only in the future, but even right now.

O.J.M.

Lord of the Hereafter

Imagine the small parade of a not too promising, and not too sophisticated group of ordinary people. Some cut branches from the trees along the road and lay them in the path of a man riding on a colt. Others take off their cloaks and lay them along the path. Soon whispers from pages of the Old Testament pass from one to the other. "Fear not, O daughter of Zion! Your king approaches you on a donkey's colt." Not really understanding what is happening to them, the people begin to respond to God working in them. "Hosanna! Blessed is he who comes in the name of the Lord! Blessed is the King of Israel." Soon it becomes a "get-on-the-band-wagon" kind of atmosphere. People begin to dance about, and to shout out that the kingdom of God is about to start. The reign of the Messiah is finally going to begin and the Romans will be driven out of the sacred land of God's people.

Heaven Too

The events which followed this short-lived triumphal procession into the city of Jerusalem show how poorly these people understood what God was saying to them through his Son, Jesus from Nazareth in Galilee. Their reactions could serve as guide lines for us in our response to God communicating with us. A study of them might help us improve our prayer of hope, hope in the hereafter, for this is where these people went wrong. Last Sunday we looked at our response of hope in this life, in the right now. We asked that we all try to deal with present problems with a prayer of hope for the now. Today we must look at the other side of the coin. How does hope for the hereafter influence our lives? What is our response to God communicating eternal life to us?

The problem is a sort of "all-this-and-heaven-too" situation. The people in the first Palm Sunday procession wanted a strong, kingly ruler and a government that would make the Jewish nation the conquerors of the whole world. They were unable, or unwilling, to look beyond their own time. When the procession lost its momentum, and nothing more happened, they drifted away. They concluded that nothing much was going to come of this Jesus of Nazareth and his idealistic teachings. So, it was not difficult for them, on the following Friday, to turn against Jesus. The climax of this rejection is found in the Passion account read today, especially in the words, "Crucify him!" What a way to respond to God entering their lives and offering them the promise of eternal life! Even in his trial before Caiaphas when Jesus spoke the truth, he was condemned as a blasphemer. We need God's truth. We need to know with certainty: "Soon you will see the Son of Man seated at the right hand of the Power and coming on the clouds of heaven." It is true we do not easily understand the Jewish figure of speech in which Christ spoke, but nevertheless the truth is that, through Christ, we are to live forever.

Long Term

In St. John's account of Palm Sunday, he uses all sorts of literary devices to have the early Christians learn the full meaning of this event. They are somewhat complicated, and it takes a scripture scholar to unravel them. The word to use for John's approach to this problem is "eschatological." The word means "at the end of time," or more simply "looking from now into the hereafter." It's the "long term" view of life versus the "short term." The Christian lives his life fully and completely in this world, but with an eye on eternity. The person who "cops out" on either one is not living his life fully, no matter

how successfully he may deceive himself. Judas is a good example in today's account of the Passion. Judas took the "short
term" view of the situation. Jesus had failed to set up a kingdom.
So Judas rejected him, and made what he could out of the
shambles, thirty pieces of silver, the price of a slave. For Judas
the "short term" did not pay off.

Christ our King

We must not fall prey to the "short term" view of life.
In this Mass we should pray for the grace to see through all
the problems and duties of this life to the person of Jesus who
gives the promise of eternal life. Let us hail Jesus as our King
and recognize that he is Lord of both the here and the hereafter.

O.J.M.

Lord of Life

Mary Magdalene came to the tomb early in the morning. Hers had been a night of weeping for the loss of him who had reached out to her in her misery and given her comfort and hope. She would have followed him to the end of the world, but now she feared that for her the world itself had ended.

Empty Tomb

She had responded to his loving forgiveness by a complete change of heart. Because of him she had begun a new life. Perhaps on that Sunday morning, however, in the confusion of her sorrow she was wondering whether life itself were still worth living. Though she was looking for a dead body, not a very bright prospect, God was leading her to the light of a great truth. At first Mary thought she had found not even a dead body but only an empty tomb. She ran off in tears to tell Peter and John that the Lord had been taken away. Later, still not understanding, she returned to the tomb. Then it happened. She saw Jesus standing there. Through her tears she did not recognize him. He asked her, "Woman, why are you weeping? Who is it you are looking for?" She took him to be the gardener, and said, "Sir, if you are the one who carried him off, tell me where you have laid him and I will take him away." Jesus said one word, "Mary." With that, God's grace flooded her mind and she knew that Jesus had risen as the Lord of Life.

The Grave

On this Easter Sunday we are like Mary Magdalene in that

we too are moving toward a tomb, our own! From the moment we began life in the darkness within our mother's body we were on our way toward the darkness of the grave within mother earth. Death is inevitable. Since for many that is not a very bright prospect, our society is reluctant to admit the fact of death. We attempt to cover it over with euphemisms and pretense: no one ever dies; he "passes away." A corpse in the mortuary must be made to look, not dead, but only asleep. Still we cannot escape the reality of death. Face death we must, but we should do so in the light of Easter Sunday.

The Empty Tomb and Our Grave

On this Easter Sunday the empty tomb of Jesus tells us something about our own grave. There was a tomb for Jesus because he had really died. But that tomb was found empty on Easter morning because he had truly risen. What happened on Good Friday and Easter Sunday has great implication for us, because dying Jesus destroyed our death, and rising he restored our life. Death is not the end of the world for us. Jesus has gone before us in death to lead us to eternal life. We are going to die some day, but when Jesus comes again in glory our grave will be found empty, not because our body will have undergone the corruption of death, but because we will have risen with Christ to the glory of everlasting life.

When Christ our life appears, then we shall appear with him in glory. That is what Easter is all about. Easter asks us to make an act of faith in Christ rising from the tomb as the Lord of Life. It urges us to hope that we too shall some day rise with him. It promises us the complete fulfillment of our lives in eternal union with God.

An anonymous poet has summed up the meaning of Easter for us in these simple verses:

> In some future time,
> maybe a thousand years,

69

maybe tomorrow,
we will know a life sublime,
no more tears,
no more sorrow.
We will stand on some high hill
and see a world
made beautiful by God,
Who came to kill
all hatred—sword and rod.
And we will live
accordingly.

O.J.M.
C.E.M.

Not Seeing, Yet Believing

We have a saying that seeing is believing. It is an expression of our practical, hardheaded approach to life, the "show-me" attitude. It can also be a cruel saying, for it implies a lack of trust in another. At first glance, the doubting Thomas of today's gospel manifested a lack of trust. He wanted to see before he would believe.

Doubting the Right Thing

And yet we should not be too hard on Thomas. At least he was doubtful about the right thing: whether Jesus had really risen from the dead and was actually alive. Everything that Jesus said and did centered around the fact of whether he could overcome death. If Jesus had not come back to life, despite all the wonderful things he had done while alive, he would not have been essentially different from any other man. All the miracles that Jesus worked were done ultimately to show his power over sin and its effect, which is death. He came to give life, but not just the human life that parents give their children. That kind of life has to end for all of us. He came to give a life that will never end, an eternal life of happiness and peace. Thomas was not willing to believe in Jesus as the eternal life-giver until he was sure that Jesus had overcome sin and death in his own person. He saw and touched the wounds; he knew by this that the person before him was really the Jesus who had been crucified. And by the signs of life he saw that Jesus was really alive again.

71

Letter of Peter

St. Peter says to us in his letter: "Although you have never seen him, you love him, and without seeing you believe in him. . . ." We live in an age of faith, a time of believing without seeing. As important as the resurrection appearances are as a testimony from the early church, it all comes down to the fact that God has given us a gift of faith to respond to the truth of the gospels. Many people have read the gospels without receiving faith from them, but thanks be to God that we have received faith. And Jesus says in the gospel, "Blest are they who have not seen and have believed."

The Effect of Faith

Faith is more than just accepting the truth of the resurrection. Through our faith we come into contact with Jesus. Our contact is not by touching the wounded hands and feet of Jesus, but by receiving from the wounded and risen Jesus the gift of divine life, especially in the sacraments. Easter, which we are still celebrating, centers around three sacraments. The first is Baptism. Again in his letter St. Peter tells us that God "in his great mercy gave us a new birth unto hope which draws its life from the resurrection of Jesus Christ from the dead, a birth to an imperishable inheritance. . . ." Baptism is indeed the sacrament of Christian birth. By it we first received that divine life which is in Jesus. We received it as a seed, something that has to be nourished so that it may grow and develop. And so the second sacrament of Easter is the Holy Eucharist.

The Eucharist and Penance

Holy Communion is meant to develop within us the seed of eternal life. In this Mass we will receive the resurrected, glorified Christ. His resurrected body is both a sign and a pledge of our own resurrection from death to eternal life.

The third sacrament of Easter is penance. According to today's gospel, Jesus on the night of the resurrection breathed on the Apostles and said, "Receive the Holy Spirit. If you forgive men's sins, they are forgiven them." Catholic tradition (DB 920) has rightly seen in this occasion the origin of the sacrament of penance. The sacrament of penance restores within us the life of the resurrected Christ if we lose it by mortal sin, and heals the disease of venial sin which interferes with the growth of that life within us.

Not Seeing, Yet Believing

In these three Easter sacraments we cannot see Jesus with our bodily eyes. We cannot touch Jesus with our bodily hands. Faith makes all the difference. We come to these sacraments without seeing and without feeling, and yet with faith we can cry out with Thomas, "My Lord and my God." And Jesus responds, "Blest are you who have not seen and have believed." Indeed we are blest, that is happy and fortunate, for our faith has put us into contact with the risen Jesus, the giver of eternal life.

Importance of Faith

A few moments ago we were all standing to hear the gospel, the word of God to which we have responded in faith. Both the power and the purpose of the gospel are summed up in the final words we heard: "These things have been recorded to help you believe that Jesus is the Messiah, the Son of God, so that through this faith you may have life in his name."

C.E.M.

73

Suggested acclamation: "Lord by your cross and resurrection you have set us free. You are the Savior of the world."

While on the Journey Home

Americans are probably among the most traveled people in the world. Most of us like to go places and see things. Possibly even now you are thinking about the summer and looking forward to some trip you would like to take. A trip helps us to get away from things and to forget our problems. But we really cannot afford to get too far from reality. We must return home to the business of everyday living, and get things back into perspective.

Perspective

The engaging story we have just heard in today's gospel is about two men who had lost their perspective while on a journey. A good guess is that they had gone to Jerusalem from their home in Emmaus to celebrate the feast of the Passover. While in Jerusalem, they either witnessed or at least heard about the death of Jesus. It was a great blow to them. They had hoped that Jesus would be the answer to their problems. Despite the astonishing news that the tomb of Jesus was found empty, they failed somehow to put two and two together. Apparently all they could think of was that their hopes had been crushed with the death of Jesus on the cross. All of life was out of perspective for them.

Breaking the Bread

Jesus seemed disappointed at their lack of sense. Then with supreme patience he explained the meaning of the scriptures, that the Messiah had to suffer and die in order to enter into his glory, that his death was the means for achieving the salvation of the world. When Jesus broke the bread at table, they recognized him and saw that he was alive. They realized that Jesus had been raised, that their hope in him had not been ill-founded, that he was indeed the savior of the world. At Emmaus they got things straightened out; they regained their perspective on life and its meaning.

The Mass

Some think that the bread Jesus broke in the home at Emmaus was the Eucharist, but it probably was not. After Jesus had instituted the Eucharist on the previous Thursday at the Last Supper, he left its celebration to his followers with the command, "Do this in memory of me." However, it does seem that the author of the gospel wanted his readers to think of the Eucharist when they read or heard this story because by the time the gospel was written the expression, "the breaking of the bread," had become a Christian term to signify the Eucharistic celebration, and more importantly because at Mass much the same thing happens as occurred at Emmaus.

According to the gospel story Jesus recounted what the Scriptures had to say about himself. He then explained their meaning. In breaking bread he not only shared a meal with the two men but also revealed himself to them. Here at Mass every Sunday we hear the Scriptures read. They are explained in the homily. In our "breaking of the bread," our spiritual meal, Jesus presents himself to us as the one who passed through death to glory and thereby attained our salvation.

On the Journey Home

Like the men in today's gospel we too are on a journey. Our real home, our lasting home, is with our Father in heaven. Also like the two men we can lose our perspective while away from home; we can get out of touch with reality, lost in the distractions of everyday life, and become confused and discouraged. We need our own personal Emmaus, a place where we can get things straightened out again.

Our Emmaus

The Mass, the "breaking of the bread," is our personal Emmaus. We come here to Church as we travel through life to heaven. In the Scripture readings we learn many different things about Jesus, but they all really add up to what we have heard today in the first two lessons. The first lesson records a sermon of St. Peter wherein he proclaims: "God freed Jesus from death's bitter pangs and raised him up again." That idea St. Peter developed in his first letter, our second lesson today. He points out that the death of Jesus was our salvation: "Realize that you were delivered from the futile way of life your fathers handed on to you, not by any diminishable sum of silver or gold but by Christ's blood beyond all price. . . . Your faith and hope, then, are centered on God."

After the consecration today you will be asked to make this acclamation: "Lord, by your cross and resurrection you have set us free. You are the Savior of the world." That acclamation will be your way of recognizing Jesus as did the two men at Emmaus.

Getting Things Straight

As we journey through life with all of its problems and distractions we can certainly lose our perspective. Every Sunday Jesus invites us to Mass wherein he speaks to us and reveals himself so that we can get things straight again. Indeed the Mass is our personal Emmaus.

C.E.M.

God Communicates

Our first reading today is basically a sermon preached on the day of Pentecost. Peter stood up with the Eleven, raised his voice, and addressed the people. Here was God on the very day of Pentecost breaking into the lives of these people through the voice of Peter. Peter proclaimed, "Let the whole house of Israel know beyond any doubt that God has made both Lord and Messiah this Jesus whom you crucified."

Response

Most of the large crowd listening to Peter had seen Jesus or had at least heard about him. Some had even witnessed his miracles. But apparently they had failed to let God get through to them. Fortunately for them, God refused to give up, as he continued to communicate his truth through the words of Peter. When the people heard this preaching of Peter, they were deeply shaken. They asked Peter and the other apostles, "What are we to do, brothers?" When they finally realized the evil they had been responsible for, they sought forgiveness, and were willing to do whatever God asked of them. Some three thousand persons were baptized on that occasion.

God Perseveres

God continues to break in on our lives. He never gives up on us. Remember the famous painting of Christ knocking at the door of a house with no latch or doorknob on the outside? When the artist was asked whether he had forgotten something in the painting, he replied that the door was the door of the human heart and could be opened only from the inside. God keeps knocking until we open.

The Bible

One way in which God continues to communicate with us is through the pages of the bible. The Vatican library has a bible two feet thick, and another an inch square. Guides jokingly tell visitors that the big bible contains everything Eve said to Adam, and the little one everything Adam said to Eve. Of course, this is not the truth. Both bibles contain what God has said—not everything, but those things that God said which were written down. Truths spoken by God and written down centuries ago are repeated in the Mass as being spoken to us for the very first time. In the Mass these truths are applied to our lives, and to them we must respond with an eager openness, as did the people on Pentecost. And God keeps working at it. He will never tire Sunday after Sunday of communicating his truth to us in the pages of sacred scripture.

Other Ways

There are other ways God uses to get through to us. Think about all the good things in your experience: life itself, your ancestors and family, the world in which you live, someone who loves and trusts you, and many other good things. All of these good things are God's communication. Think too about today's gospel presentation of Jesus as the Good Shepherd. Give a lot of thought to this figure of speech, Christ the Good Shepherd, and try to realize the many wonderful things he does for you under this title, the Good Shepherd. It's a beautiful way of saying that God breaks into your life to reveal his love to you.

Now turn to the things you consider evil in your life: suffering, sin, sickness, failure, and so forth. God permits these things to happen, but he never fails to draw good from them, if we give him the chance. The people whom Peter spoke to had missed their chance while Christ was on this earth among them, but God gave them the opportunity to grow from that experience through a profound repentance. God even allowed evil men to be the instruments of his son's death so that all of us could live, dead to sin, in accord with God's will. By his wounds we were healed. Many times God breaks into our lives through the means of apparent evil since we will not always respond to him when we are not in trouble.

Our Response

God is responsible for the good in your life, and he permits evil only that good may come from it. To the good you must respond with praise and thanks. And yet it is *always* right to give him thanks and praise, even for evil. The expression, "Oh, my God!" uttered when we've heard some tragic news can be turned into a prayer if we realize that God has only a good purpose in mind.

Faith

Through faith we must hear God's communication to us in the Mass as words addressed personally to us here and now. But our faith must go further. We must see God's communication to us in both the good and the bad in our lives. To all this communication we must respond with thanks and praise and with a willingness to change our lives as we ask, "What are we to do, Lord?" God will never give up on us. He will continue to knock at the door of our hearts until we open to him.

O.J.M.

Take Time

When do you get enough time to pray? Picking up after the children, getting the washing and ironing done, cooking the meals, cleaning the house—these things don't leave much time for prayer. Getting to work, doing the job, finishing up, getting home—these things don't leave much time for prayer. Each person, I am sure, has his or her own list of things that interfere with time for prayer. Yes, even priests and sisters and brothers have their lists. I have mine and you have yours. And the Apostles had theirs. "It is not right for us to neglect the word of God in order to wait on tables." One would think that whatever the Apostles were doing would be good and necessary. But they did not feel that way. From Christ they had learned the importance of prayer, of a life of prayer, and so they were able to see that when they did not pray enough things did not go as they should. This has been our experience too.

The Deacons

So, the Apostles proposed that several men be selected to assist them. "This will permit us," they argued, "to concentrate on prayer and the ministry of the word." A nice solution for them. But whom are we going to get to assist us so that we can have some time for praying? This is a good question. I hope we don't turn it off because we believe that we do not have the obligation to pray as the Apostles did. If we feel that we do not have as much reason for prayer as they did, then we missed the second reading of this Mass. Listen again. "You, however, are a chosen race, a royal priesthood, a consecrated nation, a people he claims for his own to proclaim the glorious works of the One who called you from darkness into his marvellous light." These qualifications are not those of the priesthood or religious life. They belong to each one of us by our baptism. Your proclaiming of the glorious works of God may be limited to your family, your school, the place where you live and work. But it is none the less real. You need the time to listen to God each day and to respond to the best of your ability. So, then, accepting the principle that prayer must be a part of our lives as Catholics, let us see what the possibilities are.

God Is There

Just before he died Father Thomas Merton made some good observations concerning prayers. What I am about to say is based on his remarks. If you want a life of prayer, the way to get it is to pray. You start where you are and you deepen what you already have, and you realize that you are already there. Jesus said to Philip, "How can you say to me, 'Show us the Father'? Do you not believe that I am in the Father and the Father is in me? The words that I speak are not spoken of myself; it is the Father who lives in me accomplishing his works" (Gospel of today's Mass). One of the first things about having time to pray is to pray where you are and at what you are doing. It's not a question of words, but rather of an attitude of mind toward God. Just as God through Christ was present to the Apostles in the gospel of this Mass, so is he present to us. We should make sure that we don't miss him right with us by looking for him someplace else. Maybe you have that plaque in your kitchen called "A Kitchen Prayer" and beginning, "God of Pots and Pans. . . ." God is with you in the kitchen, in the office, on the street, with your friends, as you shop, when you dance. Yes, even when we sin. God is there. We don't have to look for him, merely turn our minds toward him. And he's there in the alcohol and drugs and dope. Let's not be like the apostle Philip and miss the obvious.

Making Time

Another thing about prayer, if we really want it, we'll have to give it time. We must slow down to a human tempo and we'll begin to have time to listen. As soon as we listen to what's going on, things will begin to take shape by themselves. The opening words of Jesus to the apostles as recorded in the gospel of this Mass are extremely important here. "Do not let your hearts be troubled. Have faith in God and faith in me. In my Father's house there are many dwelling places; otherwise, how could I have told you that I was going to prepare a place for you? I am indeed going to prepare a place for you, and then I will come back to take you with me, that where I am you also may be." If we really believed in this promise of Christ, made to us as well as to the apostles, a lot of the hustle and bustle would go out of our lives.

Hustle and Bustle

And that seems to be the point. It's the hustle and bustle mostly that interferes with our prayers. We must approach the whole idea of time in a new way. We are free to love. And we must get free from all imaginary claims. We live in the fullness of time. Every moment is God's own good time. We don't have to rush after what we seek. It is there all the time, and if we give it time it will make itself known to us. Much of our rushing around all day long and collapsing in a heap at night is due to our desire for personal fulfillment. This is not a bad desire in itself. Nor is it wrong for parents to have that wish for their children. It's how we go about it. The wrong idea of personal fulfillment is promoted by commercialism.

Father Merton puts it this way: "They try to sell things that no one would buy if he were in his right mind; so, keep him in his wrong mind." There is a kind of self-fulfillment that fulfills nothing but our illusory selves. What truly matters is not how to get the most out of life, but how to recollect yourself so that you can fully give yourself. It's something like living in a desert. The desert becomes a paradise when we accept it as a desert. The desert can never be anything but a desert if we are trying to escape it. But once we fully accept it in union with the passion of Christ, it becomes a paradise.

Sacrifice

Idealistic? Yes. But unless we strive for time in which to communicate with God, we are never going to establish the lines of communication with those with whom we live, not even with our own inner selves. Any attempt to renew our lives, our atmosphere, our lands, lakes, oceans, cities, countryside, ourselves, is going to have to include the element of sacrifice, uncompromising sacrifice. Many things that seem important in our society will have to be given up, if we are to slow the tempo of life sufficiently so that we can think, and observe, and listen, and pray. And that takes sacrifice. Maybe we can begin by uncluttering our minds and hearts in this Mass, the supreme sacrifice of Christ. It is through him that we come to the Father.

O.J.M.

Simple Prayer

In the gospel we saw Jesus taking the apostles as they were and where they were. They were mixed up, puzzled, confused, and frustrated. They were particularly concerned and distraught because Jesus had said that he would have to leave them. They were suffering the terrifying human fear of being left to face life all alone. There is scarcely anything more frightening than the thought of having to grapple with the problems of human existence all by yourself, with no help, no guidance, no consolation from anyone else. It is the fear felt by the widow without her husband, as her children have gone from home to live their own lives. It is that terrible illness, called "homesickness," experienced by the young person who has left home for a strange, new school. It is the terror of the small child lost on a camping trip.

Not Alone

Jesus understood how his apostles felt. He wished to make it clear that their fear was groundless as he said, "I will ask the Father and he will give you another Paraclete—to be with you always. . . . I will not leave you orphaned; I will come back to you." We can see one example of the fulfillment of Jesus' promise in today's first lesson. Even after his ascension Jesus did not abandon the people of Samaria, in whose region he had worked miracles during his public ministry. His help to them came from Philip, the deacon, who was acting on the impulse of the Holy Spirit, as he responded to Christ's command to preach the gospel. Philip left Jerusalem for Samaria. There his preaching met with immediate success. When further spiritual help beyond baptism was needed, that is, the giving of the Holy Spirit by the laying on of hands, Philip had Peter and John come to Samaria and confirm the new converts.

What happened in Samaria has continued down through the centuries. The promise of Jesus has also been fulfilled in us. We too have received the Holy Spirit, and because of him we are not left alone. Through the power of the Holy Spirit the Father and the Son are present within us. But we have to find God even within ourselves. We have to search him out. We must respond to his presence within us. In a word, we must pray.

The Mass

If we have the idea that real prayer is only for mystics, or that prayer must be a very complicated formulary with just the right words of theological precision, we should rid ourselves of that notion. Simple prayers are good prayers. Exalted though the Mass truly is, even here we find simple prayers and we learn just what earnest, sincere prayer should be.

We begin the Mass with the sign of the cross, "in the name of the Father and of the Son and of the Holy Spirit." Prayer begins with a recognition of God and should include an awareness of his presence within us. Most assuredly we stand unworthy before God because of sin. At the very outset of each Mass we are asked to realize our sinfulness. At my invitation we all bowed our heads and tried to prepare ourselves to celebrate the sacred mysteries. As a group of people trying to offer God suitable worship we humbly asked forgiveness of our sins. That is a theme which continues as we pray "Lord, have mercy"; just before communion we repeat this plea for mercy in the "Lamb of God" and in the words, "Lord, I am not worthy to receive you, but only say the word and I shall be healed."

Throughout the Mass we turn to God for help in all the many prayers of petition, especially the Prayer of the Faithful, as well as in the presidential prayers at the end of the entrance

85

rite, the preparation of the gifts, and the communion rite. Each Mass itself is a total prayer of praise and thanksgiving as the very word "eucharist" signifies.

Simple Prayer

Even this sketchy survey of the Mass should help you to see that the prayer of the Mass is basically very simple. "God help me . . . forgive me . . . thank you"—in essence that is our prayer. These are the simplest and most fundamental of prayers. They help us to be ourselves before God, and they have the advantage of beginning right where we are with God. Simple prayer will help us to find God so that we need not be left alone in the struggle of life. Our prayer at Mass must carry over into the other activities of our lives. Take the time and make the effort to continue prayer through the week right where you are at any time. In your mind and heart, if not on your lips, say "God help me . . . forgive me . . . thank you." Of course your own words are best, but these three simple ideas are what make up good prayer.

It is indeed a terrifying experience to be left all alone in life. Because of God's presence within us, we need not have that experience if we learn to turn to God with simple, earnest prayer in all the aspects of our lives.

O.J.M.
C.E.M.

Through Him

The picture we get from the readings today is a truly magnificent one. It is summed up in our response verse: "God mounts his throne to shouts of joy; a blare of trumpets for the Lord." Some eastern kingdoms still preserve this ritual of the monarch ascending his throne, with the blare of trumpets, and all his subjects bowed down to the ground in homage. This kind of scene as an image of God had a great appeal for the New Testament writers. And so they present us today with a view that is highly poetic and figurative. The ascending of Christ to the right hand of his Father must be interpreted in the light of Christ's final words to his apostles: "And know that I am with you always, until the end of the world."

Why Looking Up?

The question of the two men dressed in white is most pertinent here. "Why do you stand here looking up into the skies?" The poetic figure of speech of God being "up there" serves the purpose of uplifting and inspiring us. But we must always keep in mind that Christ is our Emmanuel, God with us. It is not so much a place that Christ occupies as it is a position. As we heard in the second reading, God has raised Christ from the dead and seated him at his right hand in heaven, high above all of creation.

Head of the Church

The position Christ holds, rather than the place where he is, is emphasized in the final sentence of that reading: "He has put all things under Christ's feet and has made him thus exalted, head of the church, which is his body. . . ." Because Christ has the position of head of his body, the church, we who are his body have importance too. Never can we stress too much what our baptism has done for us. We have become a part of Christ, a member of his body.

Through Him

It is because of Christ's superior position that our prayers through him are heard. We are familiar enough with the formulary of the Mass, "through Christ our Lord." Perhaps we make it so much of a formulary that our prayers become merely words on our lips. We need to think about the meaning of this formulary. It is through Christ that the Spirit comes to us, and it is the Spirit of God who grants us the wisdom and insight to know God clearly so that we pray for those things that we ought. It is through Christ that our prayers are answered. Let us try to keep this in mind when we come to the climax of the eucharistic prayer of this Mass: "Through him, with him, in him, in the unity of the Holy Spirit, all glory and honor is yours, almighty Father, for ever and ever."

Confidence in Prayer

Notice the connection between this "through him" prayer, and the words that immediately follow it in the Mass: "Let us pray with confidence to the Father in the words our Savior gave us." This confidence that God hears us should be one of the results of Christ's ascension. If Christ had not entered into his glory, then maybe we would have some grounds for doubting that God hears our prayers. Listen again to these magnificent words of Paul in today's second reading. "May he enlighten your innermost vision that you may know the great hope to which he has called you, the wealth of his glorious heritage to be distributed among the members of the church, and the immeasurable scope of his power in us who believe." What a magnificent vision of hope. We must not let this vision become dull. It will always be bright if we believe that it is through the glorified Christ that our prayers will be heard.

O.J.M.

Rejoicing, with a Difference

On Easter and the following Sundays we hear a lot about rejoicing in the liturgy, and the Masses of the season are characterized by an expression of joy, the one word, "Alleluia." What is the jubilation all about? Why, the resurrection of Christ, of course! The resurrection of Christ should fill our hearts with joyful "Alleluias" because it is the cause of Christian hope and confidence about our own future. We have the belief that as Christ was raised from the dead to the fullness of glorified life, so we too will be raised.

Slightly Hollow

But if the truth were to be told, for many of us the "Alleluias" have a slightly hollow ring, and the joy we hear about is something we don't always feel. It isn't that we don't have faith or hope. It's just that the resurrection of Christ seems so far in the past and our own resurrection so far in the future. And the joyful "Alleluias" in church are often droned out by the dissonant clangor in our everyday world.

Today in the second reading we heard that familiar word, "rejoice" once again. But wait a minute. There was a difference. Let's go back and look at that reading again. "Rejoice insofar as you share in Christ's suffering." That really is rejoicing with a difference, a difference so great that it seems a little crazy. Who wants to be happy about suffering? Yet, St. Peter insists, "Happy are you when you are insulted for the sake of Christ." And he goes on to say, "If anyone suffers for being a Christian, he ought not to be ashamed. Rather he should glorify God. . . ."

A Change

St. Peter's idea of rejoicing over suffering deserves reflection on our part.* To begin with, there was a time when Peter held just the opposite view. When Jesus said one day that he had to go to Jerusalem to suffer greatly and be put to death, Peter judged suffering and death to be so undesirable that he blurted out: "May you be spared, Master! God forbid that any such thing ever happen to you!" Later when a servant girl questioned him about his being an associate of Jesus, he was so unhappy with the implied insult that he denied even knowing Jesus. On Good Friday he was so afraid of undergoing the same fate as Jesus that he made sure he was not even around to see what was going on.

A Happening

Something happened to Peter after the death and resurrection of Jesus that changed his outlook completely. That something we are going to celebrate next Sunday on the feast of Pentecost, the coming of the Holy Spirit. It was a real happening for Peter and the other Apostles. The Holy Spirit with his gift of wisdom penetrated their minds so that they could clearly see a truth that Jesus had been telling them all along. That great truth was the Paschal Mystery, the fact that the passion and death of Jesus led directly to the glory of his resurrection. It was not that Jesus suffered patiently because he knew his passion would last only for a while and would soon be over. Rather it was

---

° That St. Peter was the author of this epistle was not called into question until the 19th century. However, arguments against Petrine authorship are by no means conclusive. In either case, since the epistle certainly reflects the teaching of the apostles, including that of Peter, it seems homiletically valid to speak of Peter as the author.

that he knew his obedient acceptance of suffering and death would be the cause of his glorious resurrection to the fullness of life. "For the sake of the joy which lay before him he endured the cross, heedless of its shame" (Heb 12:2). In other words, Jesus was happy to suffer because he knew what the result of his loving obedience would be.

Christian Suffering

Peter and the others were also given to understand that the Paschal Mystery applied to Christians as well as to Christ, that for us too obedient acceptance of suffering will lead to the fullness of life as we share eventually in the resurrection of Christ. This was a truth they practiced as well as preached, for all of them happily suffered much for the sake of Jesus. I think that all of us know that our suffering takes many forms, physical and emotional. It is not only illness that we must accept, but all the loneliness and frustration of human existence.

The important thing is that we have the Christian outlook on suffering, which is ours through the Holy Spirit's gift of wisdom. It is not like the attitude of the man we joke about who beats himself over the head because it feels so good when he stops. Rather it is more like the attitude of the student who is happy to take the pains to study because he knows it will win his degree, or like that of the man who is happy to work hard because he knows his efforts earn a living for his loved ones, or like that of the woman who is happy to get out of bed at night to care for her sick baby because she knows her sacrifice is necessary for his health. This happiness is not the glee of a little child without worry or concern; it is the satisfaction of a mature adult who knows that it is all worthwhile.

Alleluia

Let us ask the Holy Spirit to give us his gift of wisdom

so that we may have the right sense of values in our outlook on life. With that outlook our "Alleluias" need not be hollow, and we may even feel a little of the Christian joy that should be ours as followers of Christ.

C.E.M.

Renewal in the Spirit

The people gathered in the upper room on Pentecost Sunday had gone through the apparent collapse of their dreams about the Messiah. The events of Good Friday had been a terrible blow to their hopes, but Easter Sunday was a turning point. The Risen Christ gave them a new dream and a better hope. St. Luke records (Ac 1:12) that after the ascension they returned to Jerusalem to the upper room, where they waited in a spirit of prayer and expectation for nine days. Then on Pentecost in answer to both the spoken and unspoken prayers of the apostles and Mary, Christ sent the Holy Spirit. The coming of the Holy Spirit on that first Pentecost was a wonderful response to prayer. Open to God and empty of themselves, the brethren were filled with the Holy Spirit and became new men.

A New Pentecost

It may not be clear to us that the action of the Holy Spirit begun on Pentecost continues in our own times. The apostles had been told by Jesus at his ascension to wait in the city until they were clothed with power from on high (Lk 24:49). And in one sense as they waited days turned into months, and months into years, and years into centuries. The temple became a colosseum, homes became churches, the upper room became a great basilica, and Jerusalem became Rome. And when the apostles turned to look at Peter, he was no longer there, but in his place was a man called John. All were filled with the Holy Spirit and they began to talk in foreign tongues, some in Latin or English, German or French, Spanish or Italian, and dialects from Africa and Asia. Some spoke of liturgy and others of the Church in the modern world.

Old men began to dream dreams of the union of all Christians united again as it was in the beginning, and young men began to see visions of people praying to God in the Mass in their own language in an intelligent and meaningful way. There were visitors in Rome from Spain and Ceylon, from Japan and America—from all over the world. And we have heard them all speaking in our own tongue about the marvels God has accomplished.

Vatican II

Have we forgotten so soon? Don't we realize that Vatican II was a new Pentecost, or does it now seem almost as long ago as the first Pentecost? Has that new coming of the Holy Spirit upon the Church failed to penetrate our own lives? Just for a moment let's review the documents which were the result of this coming of the Holy Spirit. First* is the Constitution on Revelation, which shows that God's word, his revelation, brings his people into being and calls them together. The Constitution on the Church and the Decree on the Eastern Churches tells us who we are as the people of God. Then the documents go into detail about those who make up these people, the body of Christ; and so we have documents on the bishops, the priests, seminarians, religious, and the laity. All of us have been set free by Christ, and we wish to extend this freedom to all, as we read in the Declaration on Religious Freedom. What do we do as the people of God? Primarily we are the worshippers of the true God as the Constitution on the Sacred Liturgy points out, and we are apostles to the world as we are reminded in the Decree on the Church's Missionary Activity. As the people of God we live our lives among others in the context of society as we see in the Pastoral Constitution on the Church

*The order given is not chronological, but structural.

95

in the Modern World. Some of our relations with others are spelled out further in the documents on Ecumenism, Non-Christian Religions, Education, and Mass Communications.

The Body of Christ

In all of these documents there is an attitude which stands out, that all of us are important. The Church is not only the pope and the bishops. All of us together make up the Church, the body of Christ, as many parts go to make up a human body. And all of us must accept our responsibility as Catholics, for "all of us have been given to drink of the one Spirit." As we heard in the second reading: "There are different gifts . . . different ministries . . . different works. . . . To each person the manifestation of the Spirit is given for the common good."

If we do not go away from this celebration of Pentecost strengthened in our wills to renew ourselves, our families, and our society according to the teachings of Christ, then we have missed the significance of our celebration today. There is nothing wrong with ourselves, our families, or our society which the Spirit of God cannot renew through us.

Pray

There is no doubt that we must continue to read and to study the documents of the Second Vatican Council. We cannot afford to let those ideas die between the covers of a book. But above all we must pray for the Holy Spirit to come into our lives so that he may guide and direct us. Pentecost must become a continuing reality. Open to God and empty of ourselves we must pray: "Come, Holy Spirit." With the Holy Spirit we have the power to renew the face of the earth!

O.J.M.
M.M.R.
C.E.M.

Praiseworthy and Glorious Forever

What a wonderful greeting! It has become very familiar to us with the Mass in the vernacular. Didn't you feel at home with it when you heard it in the second reading of this Mass? "The grace of our Lord Jesus Christ, and the love of God, and the fellowship of the Holy Spirit be with you all!" Yes, that famous greeting with which we began this Mass was originally written by St. Paul. And it certainly is appropriate for this Sunday, when we celebrate the praiseworthiness and gloriousness of the Holy Trinity. And it is a delight to hear you respond to my greeting, "And also with you."

Meditation

Let us think for a few minutes on the words of this greeting, so expressive of our belief in the Holy Trinity. "The grace of our Lord Jesus Christ. . . ." (If the homilist so wishes, he can pause briefly for a moment of recollection after the following questions.) What grace? The grace of redemption, the grace to believe in Christ, so that we may not die but may have eternal life. It's the grace of Christ being in our company. As we read about Moses in the first reading: "If I find favor with you, O Lord, do come along in our company." This grace is Christ being with us in the Eucharist.

Next think on these words of the greeting: ". . . and the love of God. . . ." These words refer to God the Father. How has the Father shown his love to us? "God so loved the world that he gave his only Son. . . ." This is the epitome of all the favors God has bestowed on us, and also the starting point for all of them. Consider the great sense of confidence that

97

comes from knowing God's truth. We have principles upon which we can base our lives. We can make decisions that we know will stand up before the judgment seat of God. And when we fail, even maliciously, we know that God loves us enough to "forgive us our trespasses as we forgive those who trespass against us."

Now we come to the words, "and the fellowship of the Holy Spirit be with you all." Do we believe firmly enough in the Spirit of God? If we did, wouldn't we all be following more perfectly the injunction of St. Paul in the second reading? "Live in harmony and peace, and the God of peace will be with you." If we don't have peace in ourselves, in our family, in our parish, in our city or town, in our country, in the world, why? What kind of fellowship is it that snubs a neighbor because he is not on the same social level? Why is our union with others so superficial, and unproductive of the help others need? If we are willing to pray honestly in this way, even secretly in our own hearts and minds, God will enlighten us as to what action is necessary and will give us the strength to carry it out.

Praiseworthy

If there is ever a Mass during the year when we should shout out the praise of God, it is during this Mass of the Holy Trinity. The first reading presents God to us as one whom we can love. "The Lord, the Lord, a merciful and gracious God, slow to anger and rich in kindness and fidelity." Was our response to that first reading somewhat weak? It should have been a resounding, "Glory and praise for ever!" Later in this Mass, during the preface in honor of the Holy Trinity, let us listen carefully to these words: "We joyfully proclaim our faith in the mystery of your Godhead. You have revealed your glory as the glory also of your Son and of the Holy Spirit: three Persons equal in majesty, undivided in splendor, yet one Lord, one God, ever to be adored in your everlasting glory." Our "Holy, Holy,

Holy Lord . . ." in response to these words in this Mass ought to make the walls of this church rock with the vibrations of our loving praise of God.

Glorious

God's quality of gloriousness is impressed upon us the more we think of who God is. We cannot understand how three Persons can be one God. Nevertheless we accept this truth in faith. In the gospel Jesus tells Nicodemus, and us, "God so loved the world that he gave his only Son, that whoever believes in him may not die but may have eternal life." It is through the Spirit of God living in us that we have this promise of eternal life. The "Glory to God" of this Mass already stands as the expression of our faith. And so it is the praise we offer God for being so glorious.

Worship

For several weeks since the beginning of Lent we have been speaking about prayer. The main thing to remember about prayer is to pray, in the most natural way that it comes to us, honestly facing God as someone who loves us and whom we love in return. But our greatest act of love, and therefore our greatest prayer, is expressed when we assemble for the prayer of worship, the sacrifice of the Mass. It is here in what we are doing right now that we can express our love for God and for all those with whom he has given us to live our lives. Yes, the greeting of this Mass is wonderful, but we each need to do our part to make it real. "The grace of our Lord Jesus Christ, and the love of God, and the fellowship of the Holy Spirit be with you all."

O.J.M.

Power and Love

Imagine that you are a peasant working in a paddy in Red China. An old man cautiously approaches you and bends to whisper a single word in your ear, "Come." You look up and notice that several of the workers are slowly moving as unobtrusively as possible toward a secluded edge of the paddy. You follow. You arrive at a thicket and see that the people are lying down between the bushes in the high weeds, and you join them. The old man lies down too and props himself slightly on his elbows. Before him are a small, dark loaf of bread and a battered tin cup. In scarcely audible tones he begins to recite familiar words. They are the words of Jesus at the Last Supper and this is the Mass. Despite the misery of your existence and a terrifying fear of discovery, you are filled with the happiness of anticipation that a long-held wish is about to be fulfilled. For the first time in nearly three years you are going to receive Jesus in holy communion.

Deprivation

Such is the condition of the Church in Red China today. The story is a true one, related by a missionary expelled from that communist country. More than anything else about China he had remembered how much those oppressed people, deprived of the Mass for so long, appreciated the value of holy communion. Frequently we do not appreciate something that is easily accessible to us. We take it for granted. Sometimes only deprivation can restore our sense of values. A woman had been away from the sacraments for almost twenty years. Her family and friends were overjoyed when she finally went to confession on the day before Easter. They asked her what it was that finally induced her to return to the Church. She answered, "You cannot imagine how much I have missed holy communion; I couldn't stand to remain away any longer."

Today's Celebration

Today's celebration of Corpus Christi is an opportunity to renew our appreciation of the Eucharist, not by depriving ourselves of holy communion, but by trying to realize just one truth among many about the Eucharist. That one truth is that the Eucharist manifests the power and the love of God in a most extraordinary manner.

God's power and love have always been manifest in the world, sometimes in special ways. For example, in the first reading we recalled the power of God that fed the people of the exodus miraculously with the manna from heaven. He fed them in this way because he loved them. But how much greater is the power and love that God shows us in the Eucharist. The Eucharist is not merely a miraculous bread, but truly the body and blood of Jesus Christ. And it is not a bread that will nourish us only for a while, as did the manna, but a divine food that will bring us to eternal life. The Eucharist is a reality only through the almighty power of God, and it is a gift to us because of the supreme love of God. Only God's almighty power can change bread and wine into the body and blood of Christ. Only his love is so strong that it moves him to give so tremendous a gift.

The Day of Promise

Today's gospel contains the first promise of the Eucharist. Jesus said, "The bread that I will give is my flesh for the life of the world." St. John records that the people quarreled among themselves and protested, "How can he give us his flesh to eat?"

It is really little wonder that the people balked at the idea. As they looked up at Jesus, they saw only a man. Without faith they could not know that the words on his lips were no empty words. Without faith they could not realize that his hands were full of power and his heart was full of love.

Fulfillment

All through his life Jesus used his power as a sign of love as he went about doing good, curing the sick, cleansing the lepers, and feeding the poor and hungry. When the time came for him to pass from this world, he showed the extent of his power and the depth of his love. At the Last Supper he took bread and said, "This is my body." He took the cup of wine and said, "This is the cup of my blood." He gave us his body and blood to cure us of the sickness of sin and to be a spiritual food that would give us everlasting life.

The Mass

Today in this Mass Jesus says to us, "Come—come to the altar to receive me in holy communion." Happy are we who are called to his supper. No matter how frequently we receive Jesus we must never fail to appreciate what a great gift the Eucharist is. The priest holds the host before us to see and says simply "The Body of Christ." As we look upon the Eucharistic body of Christ, our "Amen" should express our faith in the truth that his hands are full of power and his heart is full of love.

C.E.M.

The Two Houses

Jesus told the parable of the two houses against the background of simple Palestinian living. A water supply was indeed precious, and the temptation was to build on level, sandy ground near a wady, one of the water courses which for most of the year was a trickling stream at best. In the dry season the house was secure enough. In the rainy season, however, the wady could become a torrent overflowing its banks and causing a flash flood. The simple, mud-brick dwelling built near the wady would collapse under the pressure of both water and wind in the rain storm.

A prudent man sought the higher rocky ground for building his home. Though the location was inconvenient because it was somewhat removed from a water supply, in the rainy season it proved to be safe and sound. The man who built on sandy ground was thinking only of present convenience, whereas the man who built on solid rock was preparing for future security.

Meaning of the Parable

The meaning of the parable is clear. It is easy to give shallow assent to the beautiful teaching of Jesus about love of God and our brothers, about generosity, sacrifice and service. Even unbelievers have done that. It is quite another thing to take his words into our hearts and make faith in them the firm foundation of our lives. Every Sunday we hear the words of Jesus and we profess our faith in him. But we must not let his words be

°This Sunday does not appear in the A cycle until 1978.

something we hear only with our ears or our faith be something that we merely express with our lips.

Moses

Moses, as we heard in the first reading, told the people to take God's words to heart, to wear them on their wrist and on their foreheads. Some of the Jews took him literally. They made small boxes, called phylacteries, and placed within them a parchment on which certain key texts from the books of Exodus and Deuteronomy were written.** They wore these phylacteries on the left wrist and on the forehead. The trouble with some of these people was that God's word stopped right there; it remained external and did not penetrate their heart and soul. To wear the phylacteries was easy; to live them by the words they contained was not. Those who did not live by the word of God were indeed like the foolish man who built his house on sand.

St. Paul

St. Paul in the second reading was complaining about the same problem. His point was that a mere external observance of law, without the firm foundation of faith, was no security for salvation. The faith he was speaking of was more than intellectual assent. It involved the total commitment of the person to Christ in trust and obedience. In his own way, he was saying the same as Jesus in the gospel, "None of those who cry out, 'Lord, Lord,' will enter the kingdom of God but only the one who does the will of my father in heaven."

Challenge

Today we are challenged by Jesus to make faith in him

**The usual texts were Ex 13:1-16 and Dt 6:4-9 and 11:13-21.

the firm foundation of our lives. We are being asked to live not a convenient life but a secure one. It is convenient to build our lives on the soft, shifting sands of compromise, excuse, and pretense. We can easily compromise with the philosophy that says the good life is secured by money, position, or power. We can find an excuse for anything we want to do by adjusting our consciences to suit our actions rather than directing our actions according to what we know is right. We can pretend that we will accept any sacrifice God demands of us provided the demand is not a present reality.

But if our lives are without a firm foundation, how will we stand against the storm that God may allow to buffet us? What will be our attitude on a rainy day when we have lost our job and are faced with a huge hospital bill? How firm will we be when the winds of temptation are driving us to abandon our responsibility of love and loyalty to spouse and children? How will we accept the sacrifice when our lives seem to be crumbling because of the sudden death of a loved one or the unexpected accident which debilitates us or one of our children? Will our foundation of faith be strong enough to say to God, "Your will be done"?

Now

The time to prepare for a storm is not during the height of its ferocity but in the calm before the storm. That time is now within this very Mass. It is not enough to hear the word of God. We have to pray that his word will penetrate our hearts and souls. It is insufficient to have the name of God on our lips. We must make God's will the directing force of all we do. We cannot afford to live according to present convenience. Now is the time to prepare for future security by making real faith in God the firm foundation of our lives.

C.E.M.

105

Sincerity

When the first lesson of today's Mass was composed, Israel had sought help during time of trouble by means of political alliances with foreign nations. She had made the mistake of relying on human forces rather than on God. Then through the preaching of the prophet, Hosea, she realized that her suffering was a punishment from God for sin and once again she turned to him in repentance. But her repentance was both insincere and presumptuous. It was insincere because the people thought that repentance for sin could be expressed in merely external aspects of religion, such as the offering of sacrifice, without any real change of heart. It was presumptuous because the people thought that God's punishment would last only for a while, no matter what they did, and that eventually he would relent. They took the weather conditions of their country as a symbol of God's actions toward them. They knew that the dry season (a symbol of God's punishment) was inevitably followed by the spring rain (a symbol of God's forgiveness).

Hosea

Hosea, the prophet, was called by God to bring the people to their senses. He too used the weather as a symbol, but in a different way. Speaking for God, he accused the people of being fickle by telling them that their piety was but a passing thing, like the clouds and the dew which are present in the morning but by afternoon have dissipated in the warmth of the sun.

106

That kind of piety, expressed in merely external worship, would simply not do. God demanded that his people persevere in their faithfulness to him no matter what their pressures or temptations might be. They were to rely on him and not on any merely human powers. But the people were insincere.

Abraham

How different was Abraham, about whom we heard in the second reading, from the people of Hosea's time. Abraham was given an almost incredible promise by God, that he would be the father of many nations, despite the fact that he was very old and his wife far beyond the age of bearing children. He did not protest that God's promise was impossible. He refused to be persuaded that he had to look elsewhere for help. "He never questioned or doubted God's promise" because he was sincere in his love and piety toward God.

Matthew

The same kind of sincerity was manifested by Matthew, described in today's gospel. Matthew as a tax collector enjoyed a lucrative position; his job insured a regular and handsome income. The sincerity of his devotion to Jesus was measured by how much he was willing to give up to follow him. The Pharisees, who complained that Jesus had accepted Matthew, were not unlike the people in today's first lesson. Their religion was hollow because it was based on externals only. That is why Jesus quoted to them the words of Hosea, "It is mercy I desire and not sacrifice." That word "mercy" does not mean pity. It could just as well have been translated as love or piety. Jesus wanted the sincere devotion which he saw in Matthew and not the shallowness which he saw in the Pharisees.

107

Sincerity

The question is: what does Jesus see in us? Does he see sincerity? Some maintain that the word "sincerity" comes from two Latin words, "sine" and "cera," which literally mean "without wax."* It is said that ancient Roman sculptors tried to conceal surface cracks in a statue with wax. Of course as soon as the statue was exposed to heat the wax melted away and the cracks were exposed. The sculptor had failed to work sincerely, that is, without wax. Is our piety sincere, or are its cracks covered over with wax which melts away in the heat of temptation? It is easy to put faith in God while everything is going well for us. The real test comes when God demands absolute trust, as he did with his promise to Abraham. Are we willing to let our piety be tested by how much we are willing to give up for God, as Matthew did? When we sense no demand from God, loyalty to him involves no sacrifice.

The Test

I have no idea of what God may ask of you as a test of your piety and devotion to him. But you will know when the time comes. You will find yourself saying things like, "God, why did you do that?" or even worse, "God can't love me because if he did he would never have let this happen to me." Perhaps you have already had this experience. In either case, this Mass is your opportunity to renew your absolute faith and trust in God. Try to mean the words we will say to God in the First Eucharistic Prayer: "You know how firmly we believe in you and dedicate ourselves to you."

*Though the *Oxford English Dictionary* states that this etymology is not probable, it does not seem devoid of all possibility.

Without Wax

Even as I speak to you the wax of the candles on the altar is slowly melting away, a reminder to us of what our piety should not be. Together let us pray that our piety will be without wax, that is, really sincere.

C.E.M.

God's Love is Forever

If you have ever wondered whether God loves you, you are not without company. People of all times and places, even those of the most primitive and unenlightened conditions, have believed in some kind of God. It is obvious that this world—the universe—had to be made by someone, and that someone we call God. But people have not always been certain as to what kind of God God is. Does he really care about his creation, or has he walked away, letting the universe shift for itself? Even if he does have concern for his creation, does he love *me*—personally, as an individual? That is a question even believers wonder about. And a vital question it is.

Scripture

Much of the bible has been written with the express purpose of showing that God is indeed a loving God. For example, the first reading today was addressed to the Jews as a reminder that God loved them so much that he freed them from the slavery of the Egyptians and made them his special people, a kingdom of priests, a holy nation. In the gospel we saw the God-man, Jesus, his heart moved with pity for the people who were like sheep without a shepherd. He sent his apostles out to do good things for them for one reason: he loved them. In fact Sunday after Sunday we see God's love in Jesus.

The Cross

Of course the greatest sign we have of God's love for us is the death of Jesus on the cross. The marriage ceremony in its exhortation reminds us that people are willing to give in proportion as they love. God's love is so great that he gave his own Son to us, and that Son loved us so much that he gave his life for our salvation. You just cannot have a greater sign of love than that.

People of primitive religions felt that they had to placate a god who was about to hurl vindictive lightning bolts upon their heads because of their wickedness. They offered sacrifices to their god, sometimes even human sacrifice, in order to appease him in his outraged sense of justice. It just never occurred to them that there was a God who loved people so much that he would give his own Son to be a victim of sacrifice.

St. Paul

In meditating on this Christian revelation concerning the sacrifice of Jesus, St. Paul was overwhelmed by the realization of how much greater divine love is than human love (second reading). Only in extraordinary circumstances is a human being willing to die for someone else. A good father and mother will indeed protect their child from a threat to his life at the expense of their own life, but they will not be willing to do the same for a stranger, much less for an enemy. Imagine that you arrive home one day to find that a thief has broken into your home, taken all your valuables, and murdered your spouse and children. Meanwhile near your home the police have engaged the thief and murderer in a gun battle. You arrive on the scene and deliberately intercept with your own body a police bullet intended for the outlaw because you want to die in his place. Impossible to imagine? Of course it is. Such an action is asking too much of human nature, but it was not too much for God. St. Paul in the second reading proclaims, "It is precisely in this that God proves his love for us: that while we were still sinners, Christ died for us." It is something to think about: Christ died for us when we were his enemies because of sin.

The Mass

So that we would never forget his love, Jesus gave us the Eucharist on the night before he died. "Do this in memory of me," he said. In every Mass Jesus is made present as a victim, for the Eucharistic species under which he is present are a sacred sign of the actual separation of his body and blood (cf. *Mediator Dei,* 70). Pope Pius XII wrote, "It cannot be over-emphasized that the Eucharistic Sacrifice of its very nature is the unbloody immolation of the divine victim, which is made manifest in a mystical manner by the separation of the sacred species and by their offering to the Eternal Father" (*Mediator Dei,* 115).

Love Forever

The Mass should be a constant reminder of how great God's love really is. And God's love does not change. He still has that kind of love for us. At times we may wonder if that is really true. We may feel that God has turned his back on us, that he has changed. That is precisely when we have to remember that the Mass means that God does indeed still love each one of us.

There is a verse in today's responsorial psalm which we should allow to penetrate our minds and our hearts. That verse is: "The Lord is good; his kindness endures forever and his faithfulness to all generations." God's love is not only great. It is forever.

C.E.M.

No Intimidation

Our first reading in this Mass was from the prophet Jeremiah, who was born some 650 years before Christ. That reading merely hints at all the painful experiences Jeremiah had to endure as God's prophet. When he was sent by God to speak the plain truth to his contemporaries, he met with stern opposition—to put it mildly—from the people, the priests, and the king himself. They were all guilty of abandoning the true God in favor of the practice of idolatry, and they refused to accept the God preached by Jeremiah. He was imprisoned, humiliated and finally died in exile from the land he loved.

Dangers for Disciples

Jesus did not minimize the dangers that would await his own disciples. In effect he warned them that their fate could be similar to that of Jeremiah: disdain, torture, even death itself. He told them that, no matter what people might do to them, they should not really be worried. Of course such an exhortation may at first sound glib, but Jesus had a good point. To die, after all, is the common lot of everyone. No human power can do more to a man than nature itself will eventually accomplish. So why fear death for a good cause?

Then Jesus, after telling his disciples not to be afraid of death told them to be afraid of God. It was an unusual motive for Jesus to use, but he realized that the time would come when things would get so rough for his followers that they would need every possible motive to persevere. So he did not hesitate to warn them that the only person they should fear is God, who has the power to bury both body and soul in the eternal

113

death of hell. He warned them not to abandon God in the face of human threats, because only God has the power of eternal damnation.

But Jesus apparently could not bring himself to leave his disciples with that image of his Father. As he had done on many occasions, he reminded them that God really loved them. To do so he used the commonest, most valueless creature he could name in Palestine: the sparrow, two of which sold for next to nothing. Not even a sparrow dies without God's consent, he told them. How much more precious were they in the eyes of God, whose concern extended to the numbering of the hairs on their heads. And another motive for perseverance appears: that kind of God is worth anything that may be demanded, and he is a God who will help people meet his demands.

Today

Difficulties for God's followers have not changed. They were real for Jeremiah 650 years before Christ and they are real for us two thousand years after Christ. Very likely they are going to get worse. We need and will continue to need every possible motive to persevere. Jeremiah and the apostles suffered ridicule and disdain. Perhaps you have suffered the same because in your business you have stuck by Christian principles in refusing to cut corners, not to mention the throats of your competitors, with financial loss to yourself. Maybe you have been accused of "polluting the environment" because you have brought four or five or more chidren into the world in a spirit of generosity and love. It may be that you are undergoing real torture in trying to keep your marriage and home together because you believe that Jesus meant it when he said, "What God has joined together, let no man put asunder." Almost everyone has felt the influence of the playboy philosophy which treats sex as a toy rather than as a sacred power entrusted to us by God who demands responsibility and maturity in its use.

Every day of our lives brings pressures to abandon our Christian principles: the conversation we are expected to join which drags someone's name through the mud; the attitude others want us to share that says that you should not get involved when someone needs help; the opinion some people think we dare not contradict which maintains that our religion is irrelevant and useless in this modern world. No, we don't have to search for challenges to our loyalty to the teachings of Jesus Christ. They are all around us.

No Intimidation

Remember the words of Jesus: "Do not let men intimidate you." That means: don't follow their opinions and their slogans, and don't imitate their example. Don't be afraid of their ridicule and their disdain. The very worst that any human can do is to kill you; he cannot condemn you to hell. If you are going to be afraid, at least be afraid of the right person. Fear God! Yes, fear him—but also remember that he loves you. The God whom we worship in this Mass has the power to destroy us in hell, but he is also the God who has such care and concern for us that he will give us the strength to persevere in all that he demands of us.

C.E.M.

A Christian Welcome

One thought in our minds at this time of the year is the commemoration of the birth of our country with the signing of the Declaration of Independence on July 4, 1776.* Since 1886, one hundred and ten years after the signing of the Declaration of Independence, the Statue of Liberty has stood on Liberty Island in New York harbor as a symbol of our country. Graven on a tablet within the pedestal upon which the statue stands is a poem written by Emma Lazarus, which reads in part: "Give me your tired, your poor, your huddled masses yearning to breathe free, the wretched refuse of your teeming shore. Send these, the homeless, tempest-tost to me. . . ." Today let us reflect on whether we, not only as Americans but especially as Catholics, have continued to extend this invitation to those with whom we now share this country.

A Failure

In a sprawling suburban area of one of our largest cities there are over three hundred thousand homes, yet social workers have been able to find only thirteen homes there willing to offer shelter and care to retarded foster children.** From among three hundred thousand homes only thirteen willing to say: "Send these homeless, tempest-tost children to me." Social workers admit that the reasons for their failure to place these children are many: a lack of communication as to the need, misunderstanding or even prejudice, and fear of inability to

*In 1972 this Sunday occurs on July 2.
**Reported in the *Los Angeles Times* for Feb. 7, 1971.

116

cope with the problems. But only thirteen homes from among three hundred thousand willing to welcome a retarded child! Something is wrong.

Complacency

Perhaps your reaction is that expecting people to take that kind of a child into their homes is asking too much. People have their own children to worry about; they have their own lives to lead. And maybe your reaction is such because you know in your own heart that you do not have the heroic generosity required to accept a retarded child. If you are feeling a little uncomfortable in this realization about yourself, that is a good thing. I know that in thinking about this whole matter I feel a little uncomfortable myself, and it is a feeling I need very much to shake me up a little bit. After all, we should not come to church in the hope that we will never be rocked from our complacency. The teachings of Jesus are always a challenge to mediocrity, and an attempt on his part to free us from smug self-satisfaction so that we may grow toward the mature generosity which he requires of his followers.

Baptism

St. Paul reminded us in the second reading today that by our baptism we died a death to sin. It was meant to be an end to the pride and selfishness which is our common inheritance as human beings, and a beginning of a new life of love and generosity like that of Jesus himself.

The Gospel

And so we must come to grips with what Jesus told us in the gospel: "He who seeks only himself brings himself to ruin." Selfishness is the direct opposite of the true Christian

117

spirit to which we pledged ourselves at our baptism. Selfishness in fact will lead us right back to the death from which Jesus wished to free us in that sacrament. It is no wonder, then, that Jesus begs us to open our hearts and our lives to others, to crack open the hard shell of indifference with which we have surrounded ourselves. We don't dare to get involved. We are afraid that we may lose our much desired serenity. But the plea of Jesus continues to sound in our ears: "Welcome the lowly, the poor, the despised of this world." To this plea we must not remain deaf.

Getting Practical

Perhaps the problem of the retarded children is not a very practical one because its demands are too great and the situation too unusual. Let's get practical then! How generous are we? I don't mean now with reference to the seemingly endless collections for the foreign missions and for the poor to which we are asked to contribute in church. Real generosity and unselfishness are required when people put demands on our time and our convenience. Reflect on your reactions. One day you are especially busy. You are about to leave on an important point of business when the doorbell rings. It is a neighbor who is depressed and lonely. That neighbor needs you, your time, your sympathetic ear. Perhaps someone else keeps you on the phone for a long time with what seems to you to be petty problems, but which are making him depressed and weary of life itself. That person needs your patience and understanding. Maybe a man stops you on the street. His hair is disheveled, his grey trousers stiff with grime, his shoes shabby with wear. As he asks for a handout, he needs to be given not only money but also respect and a sense of dignity as a human being. Even if you give him money, do you dismiss him with disdain and mistrust because he is poor? If we cannot meet these simple demands with unselfishness, if we cannot give a

Christian welcome to those who need our time and interest, then we will never grow toward the mature generosity required by our baptismal commitment.

Would that we could make our own the words inscribed on the pedestal of the Statue of Liberty and address them to Jesus: "Give me your tired, your poor, your huddled masses yearning to breathe free, the wretched refuse of your teeming shore. Send these, the homeless, tempest-tost to me. . . ." Those words are a reflection of the lesson taught us in today's liturgy.

C.E.M.

"Come to Me" °

During these summer months some of us travel great distances to be with friends whom we have not seen in some time. We do so because friendship is very precious and valuable. The bible says in the Book of Sirach: "A faithful friend is a sturdy shelter; he who finds one finds a treasure; a faithful friend is beyond price; no sum can balance his worth" (Si 6:14f). Yes, friendship is very precious and valuable, but also how fragile. Perhaps we find when we visit someone who once was a very close friend that there is now little to say, when before no conversation seemed too long. Where we were always at ease, we feel awkward and uncomfortable. The old sparkle is gone forever. How seldom a friendship lasts a lifetime, or anything like a lifetime. More and more as we grow older we tend to forget people who used to be so very important to us. We may send them a card at Christmas, if we can succeed in finding the address, and that is the extent of our contact. How good we were at making friends when we were young, but how bad at keeping them.

Jesus, Our Friend

There is one friend who is always constant, always there when we need him, a friend who never fails us. That friend is Jesus. We think of Jesus in many ways, each with its value but also its limitation. Jesus is the Good Shepherd who has loving concern, but a shepherd has so many sheep to look after. Jesus is the divine physician who can cure us of our spiritual

°Based on a sermon by Msgr. Ronald A. Knox, "Jesus My Friend."

ills, but a physician always has such a large number of people waiting to see him in his office. Think now of Jesus as a friend, a personal friend, especially in the Eucharist. After all, he claimed that title for himself at the last supper when he instituted the Eucharist. He said, "You are my friends" (Jn 15:14). Today he asks us to accept his friendship with the beautiful invitation: "Come to me, all you who are weary and find life burdensome, and I will refresh you."

Always Available

With a close friend you feel free to just drop in, for your friend is always available to you. Jesus wants us to think of him that way. Jesus with his infinite power and infinite love makes himself infinitely available to us. Go to communion during a Mass in a private home with only a few present, or go to midnight Mass in a huge cathedral with almost endless lines of people slowly moving toward the communion stations—it makes no difference. In either case it is the same Jesus who says to you eagerly and lovingly, "Come to me." He is there waiting for you like a person who has come to meet you at a crowded bus terminal, looking for that particular gait, that special way of holding yourself, which will single you out at a distance.

Veils

And do not complain that the friendship of Jesus feels unreal to you or impersonal because he is hidden under the sacramental veils of the Eucharist. After all, what a sense of intimacy you feel from a friend's handwriting in a letter. You readily see through the veil of words on a page to the person of your friend. Even when you are with a friend you are only hearing his voice and seeing his face. Voice and face are veils that hide the real person, and yet how easily you see behind those veils.

In any true friendship it is the person you love, not external appearances. Though the veils change as the hair grows thin and grey and the face becomes lined and wrinkled, the real person is still the same—the person who is your friend.

Faith

If we had faith, real faith, the sacramental veils under which Jesus comes to us in communion would lift and part; we would get a much greater sense of nearness to him under the appearance of bread than we get when we are with a friend under the token of voice and face. Nor need we feel that Jesus is but a distant friend since he almost always remains silent. With a true friend even silence can be filled with meaning and warmth.

The Lord

In the responsorial psalm today we reflected on what a good friend Jesus is: "The Lord is gracious and merciful, slow to anger and of great kindness; the Lord is good to all and compassionate . . . ; the Lord lifts up all who are falling and raises up all who are bowed down." And that same Lord says to us, "Come to me, all you who are weary and find life burdensome, and I will refresh you." May our faith make us realize what a treasure we have in the Eucharist, for there waiting for us under the sacramental veils is Jesus, our friend.

C.E.M.

Heed What You Hear

Today's gospel is unusual in that Jesus is presented as giving his own explanation of the parable—something we ordinarily have to figure out for ourselves. Following this lead given us by Jesus, let us together try to heed what he has said by reflecting on the implication of his teaching for us today.

The Word of God

Jesus says that the seed is the word of God. What is this word of God? You hear it every Sunday during Mass, in the lessons, the gospel, and even in the homily. This word of God is like the rain which falls from heaven; it is meant to produce fruit, to have an effect. God's word is not mere entertainment or diversion. If you watch a program on TV, there is nothing you have to do about it—just sit back passively and enjoy the program or flip the channel button until you find something you like. Some people may say that the best thing you can do after seeing a program is to forget all about it. To God's word, however, we must respond and we must never "turn it off." But people do respond to God's word in different ways.

Different Responses

Jesus visualizes several different forms of response to God's word. First are those people who let the devil take the word of God out of their hearts. They give in to his temptation to think that the Church is out of date, old-fashioned, irrelevant—that what the Church teaches no longer applies to us today. Then there are people who hear something at Mass and they

123

say, "Now that really is a good idea. I certainly ought to do that." But as soon as they walk out the front door of the church they forget all about the good idea they heard. Next are people who get so caught up in the cares and riches and pleasures of this life that deep down they prefer all these things to God. They want their heaven on earth: no suffering, no mortification, no trouble, no pain. Finally there are those who listen to God's word and respond by applying it to themselves in an effort to lead a life like that of Jesus. A good example of a man who listened to God's word and responded to it is St. Paul. God's word changed his whole life, shaped his outlook and influenced his behavior. It gave him a profound view of life, as we heard in the second reading when he said, "I consider the sufferings of the present to be as nothing compared with the glory to be revealed in us."

Our Response

What must you do to hear God's word with profit? To put it simply, the first thing you must do is to be in church on time for the liturgy of the word, the first half of the Mass. In fact the Constitution on the Sacred Liturgy of Vatican II strongly urges priests "that when instructing the faithful they insistently teach them to take their part in the entire Mass" (56). Secondly, you should realize the value and importance of God's word. As Jesus said in the gospel, "I assure you, many a prophet and many a saint longed to hear what you hear but did not hear it." Your appreciation of God's word should move you to try to see how the word of God applies to you personally and what you can do about it. As the homilist I am supposed to help you to do this, but all I can do is help. You must take responsibility yourself. Please let me be plain and blunt about this matter. You should not sit here in church and apply what you hear to others rather than to yourself. If, for example, you hear something about the need for patience, don't nudge your spouse to imply that what is being said applies to him or her and not to you. And please do not protest that a priest certainly has a lot of gall talking about something when he is just as guilty as anybody else. No priest in his right mind pretends that he is perfect or that he has no need to practice what he preaches. If a priest happens to touch some nerve of prejudice, especially in the area of war or race relations or social justice, try not to get your defenses up. If you do honestly feel that the priest is preaching merely his own opinions and not the word of God, do not complain to someone else about him. Take the trouble to go to the priest himself and try to get things clarified. Above all remember that the word of God is intended to produce fruit in your life.

Response in Mass

Actually your response should begin right here at Mass. The Constitution on the Sacred Liturgy states that "the two parts which, in a certain sense, go to make up the Mass, namely the liturgy of the word and the eucharistic liturgy, are so closely connected with each other that they form but one single act of worship" (56). What you hear in the word should become a motive for your worship of God. When the word shows how good God is, you should want to express your love for him. When the word shows that God is our savior, you should want to thank and praise him. When the word reminds you that you must keep God's commandments, you should want to express your sorrow for having failed. When the word reveals that God has love and concern, you should want to turn to him in confidence to ask for what you need. Worship means expressing your love, thanks and praise, sorrow and confidence. And the best form of worship is the offering of Jesus in the sacrifice of the Mass.

125

Heed What You Hear

Jesus concluded his parable about the seed with an exhortation that applies to us today, especially within the context of the Mass: "Let everyone heed what he hears."

C.E.M.

White Hats and Black Hats

The old-fashioned Western movies have always enjoyed popularity, and despite the realistic trend in films I suppose their popularity will continue as the old Westerns reappear on television's early or late show. One thing you have to say for the old Westerns is that they were nice and simple in their approach to life. You knew just where everybody stood. The good guys always wore a white hat, rode a beautiful white horse, and sported two pearl-handled six-shooters which never seemed to need reloading. The bad guy always wore a black hat, rode a scraggly black horse, and had to struggle along with a single, dirty looking gun which always ran out of bullets just in time to save the good guy.

The Apostles

Though the apostles obviously never saw an American-made cowboy movie, they wanted the same simplistic approach to life. They thought of Jesus and themselves as the good guys and the scribes and Pharisees as the bad guys. They wanted Jesus to ride up on his white horse and wipe out all the scribes and Pharisees in one great burst of righteousness. Jesus in his wisdom had a completely different outlook and in today's parable he tried to move his apostles to share that outlook. The wheat represented good people, and the weeds, bad people. The weeds to which Jesus referred were of a species that was indistinguishable from wheat until both were full grown. A farmer who tried to rid his field of wheat before harvest time ran the serious risk of destroying some of the wheat along with the weeds. A prudent man waited until harvest time. The point was clear. The apostles were not to make judgments about the

127

goodness or badness of people, not even about the scribes and the Pharisees. A very important point too, which the parable cannot exemplify, is that whereas weeds can never become wheat, bad people can become good. And as a matter of fact one Pharisee that we know of, Nicodemus, became a follower of Christ. The Apostles, like Jesus himself, were to be concerned not with the destruction of people but with their conversion.

Intolerance

As we study the gospels it becomes very clear that Jesus was intolerant of intolerance. He forgave the woman taken in adultery, he accepted the repentance of Mary Magdalene, and he made an apostle of Matthew, who had been a religious outcast because of his profession as a tax collector. But he excoriated the self-righteous who thought of themselves as just and despised others. Even in this parable of the weeds and the wheat, addressed though it is to the apostles themselves, there is an undertone of rebuke, for Jesus implies that to judge others before God does so is foolish, as foolish as trying to pull up the weeds before the day of harvest.

Application

I don't think it unnecessary to say that this parable applies to us as well as to the apostles. For example, one of the most diabolically inspired movements in our day is the one which pretends that there is nothing wrong with abortion. The Vatican Council in one of its rare condemnations spoke of abortion as an "unspeakable crime" (*The Church in the Modern World,* 51). We cannot condone the taking of innocent human life simply because it has not yet been born, and we must oppose abortion as we would any other form of murder. Despite all this we have no right to judge the consciences of the pro-

128

abortionists, nor must we ask God to destroy these people in order to rid the world of the evil of abortion. God wills to let these people continue in the world "until the harvest time"—to give them a chance.

Getting perhaps closer to home, it may be that a close friend or a member of the family or a priest we have known has left the Church. It is not our business to conclude that such people are weeds in the sight of God. We just can't be sure. And looking at the same problem from another angle, can we say that we ourselves always have the certain, evident sign of being wheat? Is it not true that we begin every Mass with an admission that we are sinners, that we have failed in our thoughts and in our words, in what we have done and in what we have failed to do? I don't know how you feel about it, but I for one am very glad that I will be judged, not by my fellow men, but by the God described in the second lesson, a God who judges with clemency and who permits repentance for sins.

Not Simple

It would be nice if life were as simple as the old Western movies made it out to be, but it is not. There is some good and some bad in all of us, something to make us look like wheat and something to make us look like weeds. Judgment we must leave to God when he comes for his harvest at the end of the world.

C.E.M.

129

Prospecting, Christian Style

Many prospectors came to California in the gold rush of 1849. Any one of them could have related to today's parable of the treasure in the field. The prospector was a man who had reached an important decision which influenced his whole life. He was willing to risk everything on the possibility of hitting a gold strike which would make him a wealthy man. It was a decision that required sacrifice and steadfastness.

A Prospector

Let's trace in imagination the history of one of these prospectors. The first thing he did was to decide that he was going to base his whole future on the hope of finding gold in California. He sold his farm in the midwest and began the long journey across the Great Plains, through the tortuous passes of the Rocky Mountains, and over the Sierra Madre range into the Sacramento Valley. It was a difficult journey with dangers from climate and hostile tribes. Many times the prospector became discouraged and was tempted to turn back, especially as he came across the corpses of those who had succumbed to the weather or who had died in a gun battle along the way. But his hope of finding gold moved him to press on.

When he finally arrived in California he had to spend long hours each day mining and panning for gold. From time to time he grew so tired and weary that he would squander his meager earnings on a wild evening in the local tavern. The next morning, however, his terrible hangover convinced him of his foolishness and he realized that he had much work to do before he could really relax. On one occasion he became so disappointed by continued failure that he went into town and spent several weeks in drinking and card playing. All the while he failed to work his claim. Eventually he remembered his yearning for gold and he started all over again. After more years of many disappointments he struck a rich vein. His dream became a reality because ultimately he stuck to his fundamental decision.

Christian Decision

Our lives as Catholics are not unlike that of the prospector. God has called us to share in the divine life of his Son (second reading), a calling given us in our Baptism. Our aim is to find the gold of eternal life. Somewhere in life, however, we must make a firm decision that we are going to work toward the complete fulfillment of God's call so that we may indeed enjoy eternal life with him in heaven. Our purpose is to achieve something much more precious and lasting than even the finest gold. We really have to make up our minds about that. It is a long, difficult journey through life until we reach our goal. We may become discouraged along the way. From time to time we will grow tired and weary and squander our spiritual strength on foolish things—nothing too serious perhaps—small sins of selfishness, impatience, laziness. Maybe one day we even go so far as to begin to give up on God. We may be led to such a state because of a sudden death of a loved one, a severe financial setback, or perhaps a strong temptation to violate our sexual commitment as married people or our status as single people. A serious sin for us is doing what the prospector did as he failed to work his claim for several weeks. But deep down the prospector did not really want to abandon his desire to find gold as was shown by the fact that he did start all over again, just as we despite serious failures at times do not really want to abandon God. After serious sin we have to start all over again.

131

Solidifying the Decision

All sin gets in the way of fulfilling our real purpose in life. Small sins waste our time and inhibit our progress. Because of our weakness as human beings, some small sins are inevitable, but we must still work with God's help to eliminate them. Serious sin should not be a part of our lives at all because serious sin not only prevents us from going forward but also points us in a false direction. It clouds our vision and may one day turn us completely away from the treasure we are seeking. Most important of all we must let nothing, absolutely nothing, change our purpose in life. Because sin is a reality, we must make sure that our commitment to God is firm. Solomon, as we read in the first lesson, prayed for an understanding heart so that he could fulfill his call from God to govern his people. We must pray for a realization of our true end in life and for the help we need to persevere in reaching that end.

Perseverance

Today's responsorial psalm gave us the right attitude. We prayed these words: "I have said, O Lord, that my part is to keep your words. The law of your mouth is to me more precious than thousands of gold and silver pieces. . . . For I love your command more than gold, however fine. For in all your precepts I go forward; every false way I hate." Jesus did not hesitate to present our final reward as a motive for perseverance as he spoke of the treasure in the field for which a man was willing to sell everything. We are prospectors, Christian style. If we keep our faith and hope in eternal life, more precious than the finest gold, we will find no sacrifice too great. And one day our dream will become a reality as we strike the rich vein of eternal life.

C.E.M.

132

Shadows and Reality

The story of how Jesus fed over five thousand people with five loaves and two fish is very familiar to all of us. Despite its familiarity we may easily miss the point behind it. We can get all involved in just how Jesus worked the miracle, but speculation on the manner of the miracle takes up where the gospel leaves off, for the gospel tells us what happened, not how. Moreover, though it is true that Jesus worked the miracle out of a motive of pity for the crowds, his concern went deeper than their need for physical nourishment.

We have a key to how the early Church viewed the miracle, for St. Matthew describes Jesus' actions in terms which allude to the institution of the Eucharist: "He looked up to heaven, blessed, and broke the loaves." Even as we hear the words of the gospel, our minds should easily turn to the words of the consecration in the Mass. The point behind the gospel story, then, is that the feeding of the five thousand was a sign that Jesus wanted to feed his followers in a spiritual manner by means of the Eucharist.

The Eucharist

Jesus is concerned with the totality of our lives, but his main objective is to direct us toward our spiritual destiny. That is what is uppermost in his mind for us. For example, we would be inclined to think that Jesus used bread and wine when he instituted the Eucharist because bread and wine reminded him of that grace which he intended the Eucharist to give us. But, if you think about it, it was just the other way around. When God created the world, he gave common bread and wine, food and drink, for our use so that we might understand something of the Eucharist when it was instituted. God did not design the Eucharist to be something like bread simply because bread came first in time. He designed bread to be something like the Eucharist because the Eucharist came first in his intention.*

Spiritual Reality

God knew what he was doing when he created. The end that he had in mind was our spiritual destiny, and it was that end which shaped his plans. What is true of bread and the Eucharist is true of our lives as a whole. As material bread is but a shadow of the real, spiritual food in the Eucharist, so our earthly lives are but a shadow of the real, spiritual life that God has called us to. Unfortunately too often we view things the other way around. Those things which we can see and touch and weigh and measure appear to be real, whereas they are only shadows of what our lives are actually all about.

Disappointments

The deepest yearnings of the human heart can find fulfillment only in God. If we fail to have this spiritual perspective on life, we are bound to suffer the frustration of disillusionment. For example, some people just expect too much from love and marriage. Every marriage begins, hopefully at least, with the thrill of discovery. To love another person deeply and intimately and to be loved in return becomes an overwhelming preoccupation. But the ardent affection and strong personal attachment cannot last, for no human person, however wonderful, can fill up our intense need and longing for love. Human love is but

*From an idea by Msgr. Ronald A. Knox in his sermon, "Real Bread" —an idea which, I suppose, can neither be proved nor disproved.

a shadow of the reality of loving God and being loved by him. Indeed human love can be a beautiful thing, but even its beauty is but a reflection of what can be with God. There is no need to be disappointed with the inevitable cooling of human emotion, or to think of marriage as a failure when the honeymoon does not last forever, provided we can keep in mind that everything human is but a shadow of a spiritual destiny.

Think of what you will—the greatest accomplishment, the most exquisite pleasure, the highest honor—nothing human can really satisfy us. Only God can do that, and the sooner we realize it the happier and more purposeful our lives will become.

Blocked Vision

Sin blocks our vision. It is like a huge black curtain before our eyes hiding the bright spiritual meaning of life. Faith can lift that curtain. One reason we are here today is to pray for this faith as we celebrate the Eucharist. God is patiently directing us through the shadows of this life toward the glowing reality of eternal life with him in heaven. How ardently we should pray for the faith to see the end which God himself has had in mind all along.

C.E.M.

A Tiny Whisper

Shortly after six o'clock on the morning of Tuesday, February 9, 1971, all of Los Angeles awoke at the same time. It started with a slight, ominous rumble, followed by a terrifying rocking of the earth as if monstrous buffalo were stampeding across the land. The earthquake lasted less than a minute, but in an instant sixty-two persons were dead and millions of dollars of damage had been done. Two hospitals collapsed and a freeway was tossed about like a plastic toy. That morning many more prayers than usual were directed to heaven. There are no atheists in foxholes, and there are none in earthquakes either. As Johnny Carson quipped on his show that night, "The meeting of the God-Is-Dead Society has been cancelled."

Time of Need

Of all natural calamities earthquakes are probably the most terrifying. If there is a flood, you can get to higher ground. If a hurricane is coming, you can be warned to evacuate. But with an earthquake, when the very ground gives way beneath you, you feel completely helpless. It is not surprising to us if people turn to God during an earthquake, but it may be disappointing to God—if that is virtually the only time they pray. Prayer is not some last-ditch effort to ward off an impending evil. Prayer should be a seeking for God in all the circumstances of our lives, even the ordinary, simple ones.

Elijah

This was a lesson that Elijah the prophet had to learn.

Elijah thought of himself as a failure because he could not convert his people from idolatry. In his disappointment he yearned to die because God seemed far from him. Then the Lord told him to go to the mountain because he, the Lord, would pass by. Seemingly Elijah expected a marvelous manifestation. But he did not find God in a mighty wind, or a great fire, or even an earthquake. To his amazement Elijah felt the divine presence in a breeze so gentle that it was like a whisper. Nothing could have been more simple and ordinary.

Peter

Peter had to learn much the same lesson. When he asked Jesus to let him walk on the water, he wanted him to suspend the laws of nature. He wanted a miracle as a sign that it was really Jesus whom he saw on the lake. But because his faith was not solid, neither was the water beneath his feet. He began to sink. Then he really prayed. Peter had made two mistakes. The first was to think that he could find Jesus only in a miracle. The second was to turn to Jesus in real prayer only when his life was threatened. Jesus did not commend Peter. Rather he pointed out that his faith was very weak, so weak that he thought to turn to Jesus only in what was truly an extraordinary situation.

Ourselves

Do we need to learn this lesson about prayer? Isn't it true that when everything is going well for us it is easy to forget about God? But just let some big problem arise—the grave illness of a loved one or a natural disaster like an earthquake—then we get serious about prayer. We have the feeling, "All we can do now is pray." That feeling betrays an attitude that prayer is but a last resort.

Jesus teaches us that prayer must be an habitual part of our life in all of its circumstances. A little child does not turn to his parents only when he is in big trouble. He is completely dependent on them and somehow knows that all good things come from them. He looks to his parents for food when he is hungry, he runs to them for comfort when he has skinned his knee or had his feelings hurt, he seeks solace from them when he is lonely and blue. Above all he wants to feel that he belongs, that he has their love and interest all the time.

No matter how young or old we may be, in relation to God we are like little children, and God is a Father more loving and interested than even the best of human parents. He wants us to turn to him in prayer in all the circumstances of our lives, not merely when we are in big trouble.

Daily Prayer

In this Mass, as in every Mass, we pray to God for our needs. We express those needs especially in the Prayer of the Faithful. That is good but it is not enough. Despite the greatness of the Mass, it does not exhaust our need for prayer. Every day must be filled with prayer, not memorized formulas or set phrases, but our own personal words—words like, "Father, help me to do your will, give me courage and strength, don't abandon me, protect me, lift me out of my depression and sadness." We don't even have to say the words out loud; a tiny whisper within our hearts will do.

Above all we should not need something like an earthquake to shake us into a realization of our need for prayer. If we remember that God is our Father and we are his children, we will turn to him in prayer in all the circumstances of our lives.

C.E.M.

Keep A-Goin'

The long, hot days of the summer can often be a drag as the heat and humidity drain your energy and enthusiasm. Here we are in the middle of August with your vacation probably behind you and little to look forward to. Once in a while life itself seems to be as draining as an unpleasant August day, and you need someone to give you a friendly slap on the back and say, "Keep a-goin'! It's all worth it."

Today's Feast

Today we have come together to celebrate a great event, Mary's assumption into heaven. After her earthly life Mary was taken up body and soul into heavenly glory. Because Mary enjoyed the power of Christ's redemption to the full, preserved as she was from all guilt of original sin, she did not have to wait until the end of time to share in Christ's resurrection. Certainly we should praise God for this marvelous thing that he has done for Mary. But there is more. We should also take great encouragement from our celebration of Mary's assumption.

A Sign

Mary is the "great sign that has appeared in the sky, a woman clothed with the sun."* Mary's assumption into heaven is a sign of what our own destiny is in God's plan. By our faith

---

*Though these words of the book of Revelation refer to God's people in the Old and New Testaments, the liturgy rightly accommodates them to Mary since she is the model and exemplar of the Church, the people of God.

we believe that Christ overcame death in his resurrection from the dead. Mary's assumption, body as well as soul, assures us that we will share in Christ's resurrection. The reason is that Mary is the model of the people of God. She is not only a model of what our lives should be in virtue, but also of what our lives, in body and soul, will one day be in heaven.**

Encouragement

Just before the turn of the century a man by the name of Frank Stanton in a playful mood wrote a poem of encouragement. Some of his verses were these: "If you strike a thorn or rose, / Keep a-goin'! / If it hails or if it snows, / Keep a-goin'! / When it looks like all is up, / Keep a-goin'! / Drain the sweetness from the cup, / Keep a-goin'!" That poem isn't much as literature, but it says something we sometimes need to hear. In a very real sense today's celebration of Mary's assumption tells us much the same thing. In all the distressing, discouraging days of life we should look to Mary in her assumption for encouragement. Her assumption tells us, "Keep a-goin'! It's all worth it."

C.E.M.

**Cf. Vatican II's Constitution on the Church, 53, 63, and 65.

Not an Exclusive Club

Probably you can remember that when you were a kid you formed a club with other kids in your neighborhood. You may even have had a club house of sorts where you held meetings. There really wasn't much of a purpose or goal to the club, but there was one quality that gave it value in your eyes: not everyone could belong. Membership was selective. The fact that some kids were excluded made belonging mean all the more to you. There are people who continue this childish game even after they have grown up. They form clubs with selective membership, with undesirables excluded on the basis of financial status, color, or even religion.

Judaism

Frankly it is quite a twist that today Jews are frequently discriminated against, because originally they discriminated against non-Jews. In fact this was a big problem in the early Church. The first Christians were of course Jews. Some of them believed that only Jews could be Christians, while others protested that to be a follower of Christ a non-Jew had to be circumcised and follow the law of Moses. This was the situation despite the teaching of our first reading today from the Old Testament which states that messianic salvation is offered to all who believe in the Lord and keep his commandments, regardless of origin or social condition.

141

The Gospel

The story in today's gospel was preached in the early Church to correct an attitude of exclusiveness. The Canaanite woman was non-Jewish. When she asked a favor of Jesus, he insisted that his mission was to the chosen people, the house of Israel. When she refused to accept "no" for an answer, there followed a painful scene. Apparently the poor woman trailed after Jesus, wailing and crying. Apparently too she attached herself to various disciples who looked deceptively sympathetic for a moment, which prompted them to complain to Jesus, "Get rid of her. She keeps shouting after us." Jesus remained unperturbed by this feminine storm, and resorted to one of his favorite devices. He told a parable, but with quite a sting to it: "It is not right to take the food of sons and daughters and throw it to the dogs." But like so many of her sex, the woman had the last word, and that in an argument with the Son of God himself. With quick wit, she turned the parable to her own purpose as she observed, "Even the dogs eat the leavings that fall from their masters' tables." She refused to be daunted by the harsh words of Jesus. With a womanly instinct, she seemed to realize that he was being "cruel only to be kind," for his harsh words elicited from the lady a tremendous expression of faith. She became a living fulfillment of today's first lesson, that salvation would come to all who believed in the Lord. And the point behind this unusual gospel story was that even non-Jews would share in the blessings which Jesus came to bring.

The Romans

It was a hard lesson for the early Christians to learn, but before long the shoe was on the other foot. St. Paul had to write to the non-Jewish Christians at Rome to remind them that they must not boast that they had taken the place of the chosen people of God (second lesson).

I suppose that people will protest that they have a perfect right to form exclusive clubs, but when they want their religion to be little more than an exclusive club we have a situation that is intolerable in the sight of God. God does not discriminate against anyone. He welcomes all who believe in him and wish to do his will. And so the Church of Jesus Christ calls everyone. It is indeed a sad, scandalous situation when the members of any parish refuse to welcome someone warmly into their number, whether it be because of his low economic or social status or because of his poor reputation. It is your business to make everyone feel welcome in this church, no matter how he may be dressed, or how unappealing he may appear, or what others may say of him. The fact that he comes to church must be taken as a sign that he wishes to respond to Jesus, and, who knows, his faith may be greater than even that of the Canaanite woman.

Communion and Peace

Jesus invites us to receive him in holy communion. He yearns to unite to himself all who will accept him in faith. If others are good enough for Jesus, they should be good enough for us. Before receiving Jesus together you will be invited to offer each other the sign of peace. You should offer this sign with sincerity even if you do not know the person next to you. This sign of peace is a seal and pledge of the fellowship and unity which are found in our common reception of the body of Christ.

It is understandable that children would wish to form an exclusive club, but that is not the kind of Church which Jesus Christ founded and to which we belong.

C.E.M.

The Rock

Whenever we speak of St. Peter we do not ordinarily pay much attention to his name, but his name is unusual. As a matter of fact there is no evidence that anyone had the name Peter before Christian times. Peter, you see, is actually a nickname; the apostle's real name was Simon. Since there is frequently a playful irreverence in the giving of a nickname, we may be surprised to find Jesus himself giving Simon his nickname of Peter, which means "rock." Jesus, however, was not playful; he was extremely serious. The moment was a solemn one and very momentous indeed.

The Rock

Unfortunately in English the full impact of the name is lost on us. Jesus used the Aramaic word for rock, and that word was translated in the gospels by the Greek word, "petros," from which we have derived the name Peter. But we have also kept in our language the Anglo-Saxon word "rock" to refer to a mass of stony material. In French the idea comes across clearly since French has only one word for the man's name and for rock: *pierre*. To put it awkwardly, Jesus was saying. "You are *Pierre* and on this *pierre* I will build my church."

Unlikely Name

Nicknames are given to people to describe one of their characteristics. That's why we call some people "Shorty" or "Speedy," or something like that. When Jesus called Simon, "Rock," he was implying that he was solid and firm, like something suitable for a foundation. Remember that Jesus himself said in a parable that the wise man built his house on rock so that when the torrents came and the winds blew the house did not collapse (Mt 7:25). Actually it is a little surprising that Jesus gave this unlikely nickname to Simon. After all, Simon seemed to be a person who was anything but solid and firm. He was so weak that he denied he knew Jesus. Even after the day of Pentecost he was so unstable in the question of whether converts to Christianity had to follow the law of Moses or not, that St. Paul had to withstand him to his face and remind him to follow the correct teaching (Gal 2:12).

The Foundation

And yet Jesus clearly chose Simon to be the solid, firm foundation of his Church. As our new translation has it, he said to Simon: "You are Rock, and upon this rock I will build my Church." Jesus was sure of his choice, for he went on to promise, "And the jaws of death shall not prevail against it." Jesus was confident that when the torrents would come and the winds blow, his Church would stand firm because it was solidly set on Simon, the Rock.

Despite the apparent ineptitude of Peter, Jesus was proven to be wise. His plan worked. When the torrents of persecution came pouring down on the early Church, it stood firm. When the winds of internal dissent and confusion buffeted the early Church, it did not collapse. And what was true of the early Church has been true of the Church all through the centuries, right down to our own times, as the authority of Peter has been passed from pope to pope. Some of the popes have been great men, men not only of piety but also of vision, but others have been, humanly speaking, almost totally devoid of any qualifications to lead and strengthen the Church. There have been eras of serenity in the history of the Church, but there have also been times of violent storms. Through it all, the good and the bad, the Church has escaped from the jaws of death.

Why It Works

Why has the plan of Jesus worked? The reason is that Jesus is still with his Church, especially in the person of the pope, no matter who he may be. Peter and the other popes are not the successors of Jesus, but only his vicars. There is a big difference. For instance, Richard Nixon is the successor of Lyndon Johnson as president of the United States, not his vicar. That means that Mr. Johnson no longer has any authority as president; Mr. Nixon now has it all. A vicar, on the other hand, is a substitute, a deputy. He exercises authority only in the name of another person—the person to whom the authority really belongs. And so the authority of the pope is really the authority of Jesus Christ. To put it another way, Jesus is the real rock of the Church. Ultimately he is its firm, solid foundation. Jesus by means of the Holy Spirit continues to lead and strengthen his Church through his vicar on earth, the pope.

Jesus in the Church

These days some people seem to think that the Church has become pretty shaky, but it has definitely not collapsed under the torrents and winds of modern problems, nor will it do so. The plan of Jesus will continue to work until he comes again in glory. No matter what you may think of the present pope, either favorably or unfavorably, no matter who the next pope will be or what he will be like, the Church of Jesus Christ stands on the pope as on a rock. Make no mistake about that. You have the guarantee of Jesus Christ himself that no torrent, no wind will destroy his Church, firmly set on its foundation, the "Rock."

C.E.M.

Divine Standards

Whenever you love somebody, you don't want anything bad to happen to him, any more than you want something bad to happen to yourself. However, when you take it upon yourself to decide what is good and what is bad for another person, your judgment just may not agree with his.

Prediction

Such was the situation in today's gospel. Jesus clearly told his apostles that he had to go to Jerusalem to suffer greatly and be put to death, and be raised up on the third day. The prediction of his death was such a surprise and a disappointment to the apostles that they scarcely even heard the words about resurrection. They were downcast and dejected. Then Peter decided that suffering and death were bad for Jesus, and he took it upon himself to lift what he thought were the sagging spirits of Jesus by saying, "May you be spared, Master! God forbid that any such thing ever happen to you." To Peter's utter astonishment Jesus exploded with a violence rarely seen in him: "Get out of my sight, you Satan! You are trying to make me trip and fall." Can you imagine how poor Peter must have felt, how shocked he must have been?

The Father's Plan

Without realizing it Peter was playing the role of Satan, tempting Jesus to follow the easy, human path of an earthly messiah rather than adhere to the plan of his Father. It was not an easy plan for Jesus to accept, this plan of suffering and

147

death, and Peter was not making it any easier by his well-intentioned comments. Later in the garden of Gethsemani Jesus struggled to accept this will of his Father, and Peter even then failed to understand what was going on as he slept through the whole ordeal. How little Peter knew of his Master and the lonely course on which the Father had set him, the total sacrifice of himself.

God's Standards

Jesus summarized Peter's whole problem in one sentence: "You are not judging by God's standards but by man's." Man's standards say: "Be comfortable; seek security; take care of yourself; don't overdo it." How different are God's standards! God shows in Jesus that real happiness comes through suffering, true joy through sorrow, and everlasting life through death. Jesus said that he *must* suffer and die in order to be raised up. That was the will of his Father.

Peter did not want what he judged as bad things to happen to his Master, nor did he want them to happen to himself. So, after his rebuke, he was in for more amazement and shock as Jesus went on to say: "If a man wishes to come after me, he must deny his very self, take up his cross, and begin to follow in my footsteps." The plan of the Father applied not only to Jesus, but to his disciples as well. And that means us too.

Mystery

Just *why* God demands suffering is a mystery, something that even Jesus did not explain. It is not that God in heaven looks down upon our suffering and takes some kind of twisted pleasure in what he sees. Nor is it really a question of some kind of payment for sin in the old idea of an eye for an eye and a tooth for a tooth. Perhaps we get closer to the truth

148

when we realize that suffering is the measure of a person. It shows how big he is. It can also be the test of love because we are willing to suffer for another if we love him enough. But when all is said that can be said about it, we simply must accept suffering in trust and confidence as Jesus did. That involves every form of suffering, not just the physical kind, but all the mental and emotional anguish, the frustrations, the loneliness, the boredom of human existence. Accept it all we must, but we should not be surprised if our acceptance is a struggle. It was a struggle for Jesus. And as we look up at the crucifix and remember that Jesus tells us to take up our cross, we may be tempted to say, "May we be spared! God forbid that any such thing ever happen to us!"

Resurrection

When we feel that way, we must remember that Jesus not only said that he had to suffer and die, but also that he would be raised on the third day. If we share in the cross of Christ, we will share in his resurrection as well. St. Paul, therefore, reminds us today not to conform ourselves to this age, but to offer our bodies as a living sacrifice to God (second reading). We are here to follow that advice, to offer ourselves with Jesus in the Mass. We will pray after the consecration that Jesus "may make us an everlasting gift" to the Father (Third Eucharistic Prayer). A gift is not really a gift until it has been accepted. God will accept the gift of ourselves in union with Jesus if we willingly embrace suffering and even death as Jesus did. Then we can expect to "share in the inheritance of the saints," those people who heeded the word of Jesus and took up their crosses and followed him.

God's Love

In our lives we must judge by God's standards, not by

149

6

flag and the Cross planted there were left for others to find, nor did Spain pursue those northern discoveries.

But in a sense, Spanish interests did move north. The focus now was not on Baja California, not on San Diego, not on Monterey. The focus was on San Francisco Bay. Ecela, one of the officers of the *Santiago,* was sufficiently interested in seeing the famed harbor from land to organize a party, including Father Palou. Following the route traveled by Rivera and Palou the year before, they explored the shoreline and surrounding country. Rivera's adamant decision that it was not a suitable location for a mission or pueblo did not agree with their findings, nor, indeed with those of any of the other groups that visited the area. The Ecela party just missed the *San Carlos* but found the papers left by the officers and concluded, rightly, that they had returned to Monterey.

Three Spanish ships lay at anchor in Monterey Bay at one time. This was an unprecedented event for the isolated group of Caucasians at Monterey. Implicit to a ship is an aura of romance and these three had special significance. First of all, they bore testimony that no foreign power threatened their settlements; the ships, their officers and men were links with the world from which this group had long been separated; and they directly represented the Viceroy, commander, arbiter, ruler, and sole support; furthermore, they had come in the name of the King of Spain.

It called for celebrations! Everyone was in fiesta mood. Rivera banqueted the explorers with all the pomp, etiquette, splendor and courtly grace this far outpost would allow. Serra invited them to Carmel where he spread his best table and generously entertained them with his typical affability, wit and charm. Fat beeves and lambs were slaughtered. Vegetables, fruit and berries were brought in from the gardens, fish fresh from the sea and wine, the best wines of Spain. Spirits were high and the men of the sea had tales to tell of their adventures and of the people they had seen along the northern coasts.

Serra was their most attentive listener. The natives, large of stature, well built, sturdy, agile, bearded were fairly intelligent and friendly. The Mission President sang the Mass of thanksgiving and transcendentally adopted those newly discovered people of the north. The same immutable urge that had sent him from Palma half-a-world across the sea, that same intonation from within flared anew, not dimmed but nourished by age, hardship, discouragement and distance. He spoke of planting missions all along the northern coast. Those tall, friendly people were ready to learn trades, to build, to use their dormant minds and to teach their fingers and hands new skills, new means of producing food and of living. They were waiting to learn of the living Christ, of God's love and of eternity. Why should not this project go forward? It was Spain's best assurance of safe and secure Pacific shores. But no one heard!

The days of festivity were soon over. One by one each ship set white sails against blue skies and drifted out of view. The quiet of abandoned hopes settled down on the striving community and the monotonous pattern of life resumed its rhythmical routine. Summer mellowed into fall.

Just before sailing time, Juan Perez, navigator of the *Santiago*, became seriously ill. Shipmates and landsmen pled with him to remain in Monterey but the seasoned mariner was determined to sail with his ship. Two days out of Monterey he died. A fellow Majorcan, one of Serra's best friends and one of California's most resolute and conscientious "love is the fulfillment of the law" of God. It includes every-thing, and Jesus teaches us in the gospel that part of love is to correct the faults of others.

Parents

In some situations we have a grave obligation simply because of our relationship with others. The most obvious example is that of you parents with your children. It has always been hard to get a happy medium between absolute tyranny and down-right permissiveness, but today the trend generally is toward leniency rather than strictness. You have to decide in this very complicated matter what you must do to create the proper atmosphere in which your child can grow toward mature respons-ibility, but you should never think that no discipline and no correction will accomplish this goal. Children, like the rest of us, are affected by original sin. They need guidance and direction—more when they are younger and less as they grow older. Psychologists also remind us that a child who is never guided or directed feels abandoned by his parents, even as he delights in his unwarranted freedom. Some gross misbehavior by a child is nothing more than a pitiful attempt to win a little attention from his neglectful parents. No child enjoys discipline, even well-motivated discipline, but deep down he recognizes that it is a sign of love and concern. It probably will be only later in life that he will look back and appreciate what you as parents have tried to do for him.

Husbands and Wives

You husbands and wives have an obligation to correct each other's faults, not in a spirit of nagging pettiness or faultfinding, but in a spirit of loving communication. And as Jesus says, "Keep it between the two of you." If you really think that your husband does not spend enough time at home, tell him, not your girl friend next door over a cup of coffee. If you think your wife is a sloppy housekeeper, tell her, not the boys you bowl with. Sure it's a touchy thing; sure it has to be handled delicately. But it is usually better to risk having a little fur fly and perhaps solve a problem than to let it drag on indefinitely and grow into something that pushes you farther and farther apart.

Moreover, you husbands and wives who are here together are both hearing what Jesus is saying about pointing out faults. You know that his words should not be taken as an excuse for a gripe session. On the other hand, when your spouse tries to talk about something wrong, don't fly off the handle. Remember that he or she is just trying to be a good Catholic and follow the teaching of Jesus. And of course it has to be a two-way street: when you point out the other's faults, you should be prepared to hear about your own, because none of us is perfect.

Others

This teaching about correcting the faults of others applies to all our human associations, both in and outside the family. Maybe you know that a friend of yours is drifting into an affair. Don't just gossip about that person until he or she has wrecked a marriage and then sit back and say, "Boy, I could see it coming for a long time." Perhaps someone you work with has been hitting the bottle and as a consequence is not on the job the way he should be. Don't wait until the boss has to fire him and then complacently observe, "Well, it's no surprise to me; the only wonder is that the boss didn't get on to him sooner." Or it can be that your Catholic neighbors are not going to church or are not sending their kids to C.C.D. Don't be afraid to bring up the subject. Your concern may very well change the situation for the better.

celebrate the great occasion. Everyone, that is, except Rivera.

Rivera had new problems, which left him more irascible than ever. On top of everything, Anza's coming at this time would force the issue of establishing missions in the San Francisco area. Rivera had repeatedly opposed extending the mission system beyond Monterey. Again on his return from San Francisco, the year before, he had stated emphatically the area was not suitable for missions. Despite these decisions, Serra had urged him to found a mission there. Then provoking his aggravation further was Bucareli's letter, demanding that the San Francisco missions be founded immediately. Anza's coming did not set well with Rivera.

While the ships were still in Monterey Bay and the Anza party was struggling across barren deserts, Serra had again pressed the issue of founding new missions. Four of Palou's Baja California priests still awaited assignments. Rivera's argument that he had too few military was justified on the grounds that Bucareli had not sent the one hundred men he had promised. To off-set this, Serra proposed that six of his guard at San Carlos could be spared and that San Diego could spare six more. With these men, they could found one mission at San Buenaventura. Rivera refused, but finally yielded to the *padre's* tenacious persuasion by a compromise. He would agree to founding one mission at San Juan Capistrano, half way between San Gabriel and San Diego.

Serra's persistence, aside from religious zeal, was pure logic. Time was running out: his years were numbered; the Spanish government was showing every sign of weakness and lack of funds; and colonists were coming. In other localities he had seen that the entire mission system had broken down, due to a few troublesome colonists. Now the Indians were in the mood for missions. If he could complete the California mission ladder without these long interruptions, the Indians, trained in a variety of skills, could soon cope with the inevitable influx of colonists. Rivera, on the other hand, was responsible for keeping peace among increasing numbers of unpredictable, wild savages with an extremely limited and scattered militia. There was, too, the unwritten and unspoken matter of authority. Rivera, supposedly top man, actually had authority only over a handful of soldiers. The bulk of the population, the Indians, under the mission system, were subject to the *padres*. The real collision course was one of power. The governor, regardless of name, resented the power of the *padres* and limited it as much as possible without falling into disrepute with the Viceroy. Serra, not concerned with authority wanted only to keep peace and progress with the work of conversion.

In accordance with Rivera's concession to found San Juan Capistrano, Father Lasuen (who had served under Serra in Baja and one of the six who had come with Palou), along with Sergeant Ortega from San Diego and twelve soldiers, arrived at the location selected for the mission on October 29, 1775. They raised the Cross, blessed it and said the Mass of dedication. The natives showed every sign of friendliness and even offered to help with the work. In a short time, the corral for the livestock was completed and the foundations laid for the buildings. San Juan Capistrano seemed to be to a fine start. Then word came of terror at San Diego.

Ortega and his men were to return at once. This meant Capistrano must be abandoned, at least for the time. They buried the bells and other non-perishable supplies and rushed back to the scene of trouble.

pletely, but there is a catch. Jesus tells us what the catch is: if we want God's forgiveness—and we all need that badly—then we must forgive injuries done to us. This point was so important in the mind of Jesus that when he taught us to pray he gave us these words: "Forgive us our trespasses as we forgive those who trespass against us"—words we will pray once again in this very Mass. We have to take these words and the teaching of Jesus seriously. We must be like the official in the way he sought forgiveness, but unlike him in the way he refused forgiveness.

Bigness

Jesus never tired of teaching the need to forgive others because he realized how difficult a virtue it is for us. Someone says something behind your back. You find out about it. Your indignation grows and the hurt festers in your heart. The more you think about it the less inclined you are to forgive this "enemy" of yours. Or someone insults you in front of others, or ignores you, or stands you up for an appointment. It may not seem important to anyone else, but it is important to you and you find the offense hard to forgive.

It is not surprising that we find it hard to forgive. That is the way human nature is. You see, it takes bigness to forgive. That is why it is easy for God to forgive, difficult for us. Even when we think we are very good about forgiving others, it may not be enough. Peter thought he was being very big about the whole thing when he put it this way to Jesus: "When my brother wrongs me, how often must I forgive him? Seven times?" Perhaps Jesus chuckled to himself about Peter's supposed generosity, but he made it clear that seven times was not even close to being enough. His reply, "seventy times seven times," meant without limit—as often as you are wronged, that is how often you must forgive.

A Real Test

A real test of our bigness is not only how frequently we forgive but how completely. Haven't you heard someone say, "I forgive, but I just can't forget"? Maybe you have said it yourself. That attitude—forgiving but not forgetting—is in reality far from the ideal that Jesus had in mind. To nurse hurt feelings, while mouthing words of pardon, is not really Christian forgiveness at all. We say, "I just don't want to get burned again," and what we actually mean is that we now wish to alter our relationship with the person who has hurt us.

Forgetting

Jesus wants us to practice his kind of forgiveness, the kind he not only preached but also practiced. After any injury, for which a person is sorry, nothing changes. Remember what Peter did to Jesus at the time of his passion. Not once, but three times he denied that he even knew Jesus. Before that denial Jesus had promised Peter that he would be the head of the Church, and despite Peter's denials during the passion, Jesus stuck to his promise. Jesus didn't say, "All right, Peter, I forgive you, but I just can't forget your disloyalty and so someone else will have to take your place." True forgiveness involves a kind of spiritual amnesia. That is what we hope and pray for from God and that is what we must grant to others.

Any offense against us is a mere fraction of what we are guilty of by sin before God. God will indeed write off our debt, but there is a catch. If we want forgiveness from God we must forgive those who have offended us with no limit on the number of times and with a generous act that not only forgives but also forgets.

C.E.M.

his advice and consolation and Serra could prevent drastic reprisals. Rivera, knowing this, refused a military escort for the missionary president.

Rivera's party happened to reach San Gabriel the day before Anza's arrival from Tubac. This explains Rivera's attitude upon seeing Anza. Anza, the old Indian fighter, came to Rivera's assistance. Showing force at a time like this was important. Anza, with seventeen of his men and Father Font accompanied Rivera and his ten men to the troubled mission.

By February, he felt he had served the cause of San Diego and returned to his colonists at San Gabriel. Actually, the Spaniards feared the Indian tribes of the back country, perhaps thousands, might be involved in this thing. The show of military strength may have discouraged them. However, it seems more probable that it was limited to those who had heard the fiery voice of San Carlos. At any rate, there was no further trouble.

Anza and his group proceeded northward, receiving an enthusiastic welcome at each mission with, "the festive peal of the good bells." [2]

After stopping at Carmel, they went on to San Francisco. Father Font wrote his impressions, "The port of San Francisco is a marvel of nature and might well be called the harbor of harbors." And from a vantage point above the Golden Gate, he observes, "Indeed, although in all my travels I saw very good sites and beautiful country, I saw none which pleased me as much as this. And I think that if it could be well settled like Europe, there would not be anything more beautiful ... and the harbor so remarkable and so spa-

2. All quotes on this page from Father Font's Diary, **Bolton-Anza's California Expedition,** pp. 392-5.

Betty Berg Favello

Entrance to the new Mission Dolores, San Francisco, noted for its beautiful Spanish Baroque style.

love for him, and he will give us a just reward. Meanwhile we should not be looking around to see what others are doing or not doing, or what gifts others may have from God. Every now and then we hear about the "death bed conversion" of someone who has lived a pretty wild life, and perhaps we are moved to feel that is is simply not fair. We try to live our whole lives as good Catholics, and somebody else comes along and in a few minutes makes his peace with God and goes to heaven, as apparently the good thief on the cross did. If God wants to be overly generous with such people, that is his business and we have no right to complain. After all, nothing has been taken away from us.

Sometimes we may be tempted to be distressed about people who seem to be "getting away with murder." We work hard, try to be good and to do the right thing all the time, while those who seem to care little for God or anyone but themselves prosper and have everything their own way. We may think that we are better than they morally, and yet they are better off than we financially, socially, and in every other material way. Maybe we feel not only envious of such people but also a little spiteful toward God because of their good fortune. If such be the case, we must open our ears and listen to God saying to us, "I am free to do as I please, am I not? Or are you envious because I am generous?"

Generous Toward Us

There is another reality we must face. Does God deal with *us* in strict justice alone or is he also very generous toward us? Is there anything, when you come down to it, that we can do to merit the reward of heaven in strict justice? Certainly not! Even a full lifetime of work for God is more than amply repaid with the eternal life of heaven. The greatest saints received a richer reward than they deserved. In other words, we too are the recipients of God's great generosity.

In the preface of the Mass we proclaim that we do well always and everywhere to give God thanks. We should be grateful that God is just, but we should be ecstatic in our thanksgiving that he is also generous—more generous than any human being ever could be. God's generosity, no matter to whom it may be extended, is something we should never complain about.

C.E.M.

tonio sailed away leaving the work to the unconscionably slow process of native labor.

Military reinforcements came from Loreto and Rivera had no alternative but to rebuild San Diego, reestablish San Juan Capistrano and establish the San Francisco missions.

On November 1, 1776, Serra sang the High Mass of dedication and California's seventh mission at San Juan Capistrano was reestablished. The sixth, at San Francisco, had been founded in the interim. Anza and his colonists had been more than patient. Finally, Anza returned to Sonora and left Moraga in charge of the colonists, with orders to proceed with the foundation of the mission, presidio and colony. The presidio was established in June. On October 9, 1776, three months after the colonies on the east coast had signed the Declaration of Independence, Mission Dolores de San Francisco was founded. Actually, everything but the official establishment had been done in June.

Rivera received another letter from Bucareli about this time, stating that he presumed both missions and the presidio at San Francisco had been founded. This threw another fit of fear into the commander and as he traveled from San Diego he was relieved and gratified to know the mission and presidio had been founded.

Santa Clara, the eighth mission of the chain was founded on the 12th of January, 1777 and the pueblo of San Jose, nearby, was settled by Anza's colonists.

By 1777, eight years after her beginning, Alta California had surpassed Baja in growth and stature. Eight missions were growing and prospering and California had become an institution. Nothing could stop her progress now.

Three years earlier, in 1774, Galvez had sugggested that

Josef Muench

Altar in Mission Dolores. The old carved wooden altar which was brought from Mexico in 1780, only 4 years after the founding of the Mission San Francisco De Asis (commonly called Dolores) is still beautiful and the painting on the ceiling is still the original.

in his inscrutable wisdom determined what was best for his Son, and in his infinite love gave him the highest possible personal fulfillment.

Our Attitude

We cannot always determine easily what it is that God asks of us. We have God's revelation as taught us by the Church, and we must follow it, but even this leaves many gaps for us concerning details. Our lives are a constant search for God's will. The important thing, however, is our attitude. And St. Paul instructs us today that our attitude must be like that of Christ. We are here at this Mass to tell God that we will obey his wishes. That is one thing that our offering should say. But we must not be like the son in the gospel parable who, when told by his father to go and work in the vineyard, replied, "I am on my way," but never went. Words are not obedience; actions are. Words, even the beautiful words, "Thy will be done," which we will pray in the "Our Father" are not enough. "Thy will be done on earth as it is in heaven," we will say. And how is God's will done in heaven? With perfect, unquestioning obedience. It is our attitude, then, that matters, our readiness to accept God's will for us, whatever it may be.

Fulfillment

In honesty we must admit that problems with human authority will continue simply because the authority is human. To God's authority, however, we can and must respond with perfect, unquestioning obedience. Our attitude must be like that of Christ. If it is, then we can be sure that our reward will be like his too because God's authority is competent and of good faith.

C.E.M.

Who's Rejecting Him Now?

One of the most incredible things in the life of Jesus is the fact that so many people rejected him. Would you have done so? Jesus went about doing good, trying to lead people to ever-lasting happiness. Not only did he preach the goodness and love of his Father for men, but he himself revealed that goodness and love by his actions. Jesus was disappointed by rejection, but not surprised. Rejection was part of the long, sad history of his people, a history which Jesus of course knew very well.

A Warning

Jesus reflected on the ministry of Isaiah, the prophet, some seven hundred years previously. He recalled the first lesson we heard read today, in which Isaiah gently tried to persuade the people to turn from their wicked, fruitless lives. Isaiah started with a point of agreement. He observed that a man who carefully prepared a vineyard and planted the best of vines was right in expecting fine grapes from his vines. A fruitless vine deserved only to be rooted up. Everybody had to agree with that. Then slowly Isaiah revealed the hard truth: the people were the fruitless vine which had received so much care and attention from God. Jesus took a cue from Isaiah. He too spoke of a vineyard and began with a point of agreement, but he made his lesson more personal. Instead of speaking of an expectation from the vines, he referred to the duty of the tenant farmers. It was their obligation to make a return to the owner on his investment. The slaves sent by the owner represented the prophets of the Old Testament, such as Isaiah. The son sent as a last resort represented Jesus himself. It was bad enough to

165

7

mistreat the slaves, but it was absolutely intolerable to kill the son of the owner. Jesus knew that his rejection would be so complete that the leaders of the people would kill him, the Son of God. His parable was a clear warning which was to go unheeded.

Why?

It is indeed incredible that the prophets and even Jesus himself were rejected by so many people. Why were they rejected? There are many complicated reasons, but one reason is that the truth can hurt—not indeed the truth about the goodness and love of God, but the truth that God demands and deserves a response to his goodness and love. That response means a complete change in life, a way of acting that is different. When the truth makes us face our own failures and inadequacies and our own need for change, we put up defenses. The simplest is to ignore or deny the truth. When a teacher, for example, informs irresponsible parents that their child is both a scholastic and disciplinary problem in school, that evaluation is a judgment of the parents as well as the child. Rather than face their own failure and the need to do something about the child, the parents take the easy way out and reject the teacher's report.

Who's Rejecting?

Who's rejecting Jesus now? We might say that the answer is obvious—all the irreligious, unbelieving people in the world. But it is informative to note that today's parable was not addressed to irreligious, unbelieving people. Jesus told the parable to the scribes and Pharisees, who prided themselves on the exactness of their religious observances. The problem was that their piety was merely external, not from the heart. And maybe we are the ones to whom the parable is directed today.

Please do not misunderstand me. I do not presume to accuse anyone. I merely mean that we must give this some thought, and I recognize that I too perhaps more than anyone else must give it some thought.

Demands

The teaching of Jesus is really very demanding, even frightening. Have we really listened to it or have we put up our defenses? Real listening means nothing less than constantly admitting that we have not yet put into practice what we profess to believe. Remember what Jesus has taught in the gospels just during the past five Sundays: take up your cross and follow him; have the courage humbly to correct the faults of others; be so eager to forgive others that you forget what they have done to hurt you; be content with God's generosity to others when the last come first; give God complete obedience like that of Christ which led him to suffering and death.*

Not Easy

That sampling is not an easy teaching to listen to, and so we put up our defenses. Who wants to give up comfort and pleasure to take up a cross of illness, or loneliness, or frustration? The cross seems a crazy approach to life. And that stuff about correcting the faults of others—well, just try it and you'll see that it never works anyway. As for this business of forgiving and forgetting, that's fine for someone to talk about who hasn't really been deeply hurt. And why should bad people always seem to be better off? It isn't right. And if God is so loving, how can he demand an obedience that leads to suffering and death?

*The references are, in order, to the gospels of the 22nd through the 26th Sundays of the Year.

Are We Listening?

Are we listening to the teaching of Jesus Sunday after Sunday, or have we dismissed it as impractical or irrelevant, or as directed to others but not to us? If we let that teaching come through we open ourselves to the possibility of having to change our lives. If we are not listening, then one day we will wake up to find that "the kingdom of God has been taken away from us and given to a people that will yield a rich harvest."

The truth can hurt, even the truth preached by Jesus. That truth demands that we be different from others; it requires that we accept suffering and self-denial, and that we abandon our selfishness to be generous in our love and a service to God and our fellow men. Don't think about the scribes and the Pharisees. Don't look around at anyone else. Ask yourself the question: "Who's rejecting Jesus now?"

C.E.M.

We've Been Invited

We have an old saying that a bird in the hand is worth two in the bush. This saying means, of course, that having something right now is better than holding out a hope for something more in the future. This saying may be true of hunting, but it is certainly not true about life itself.

As Catholics our approach to life is based on the belief that what lies before us after death, even though unseen, is better than what we have in this world, no matter how good or bad things may seem right now. We believe that God calls us to be happy not merely in a passing way, but forever in heaven. We are basically on a journey to a promised land. We profess to believe that heaven in the future is better than this earth in the present.

The Banquet

In today's gospel Jesus compares heaven to a great banquet.

°The story of the man without a wedding garment poses special problems if read in conjunction with the parable in vv. 1-10. One wonders how a man who has been dragged off to a celebration could possibly be expected to appear in proper attire. Some maintain that it was usual for the host to supply invited guests with a wedding garment (cf. 2K 10:22), but there is no evidence of such a practice in Jesus' day. The best explanation appears to be that the incident was actually a separate parable, and so we should not expect consistency with the previous episode. It seems better, therefore, to use the short form of the gospel which omits the second parable, rather than attempt a long explanation of how and why these two parables came to be joined together.

The imagery was not new. It was used in the Old Testament, as we heard in the first reading from Isaiah, because a splendid banquet is a good symbol of joy and happiness, as well as mutual union and love. Even in our own experience we can recall a special dinner at Thanksgiving or Christmas at which everyone enjoys not only all the fine food and drink but also the conversation and the feeling of friendship and love. As Jesus told the parable he described how the king made elaborate preparations for his dinner and then sent out his invitations. To the amazement of the king some ignored the invitation and went off to attend to business and personal affairs. To the absolute indignation of the king others rose up in rebellion against him and murdered his servants. Those invited represented both the Jewish people of the day and their leaders, some of whom in rebellion killed Jesus himself. If we did not know how the people and especially their leaders reacted to Jesus and his invitation to his kingdom, we would think the parable farfetched. Jesus told the parable as a warning to the people of his time, but also as an indication to us that we too have received an invitation, for we are the people who were later called to the banquet.

The Invitation

We have not ignored this invitation; otherwise we would not be here at Mass today. But we are still on our way to the banquet. Since we have not yet arrived, we have to make sure that we do not turn aside on the way. A danger to us is that we may allow the affairs of this life, our pleasure as well as our obligations, to blot out our vision of heaven as the real goal of life. This life, the bird in the hand, is very real. Its attractions are appealing and its duties compelling. Heaven, the two birds in the bush, seems very unreal and far away. We believe it is there and we know it is our goal, but we are not quite sure what it is all about. None of us has ever seen God, and so we cannot appreciate him. We know that he will give us an unending life of perfect happiness, but we can't get a picture of that in our imagination. Faith, and faith alone, can keep us moving toward heaven.

The Mass

The finest expression of our faith in heaven can be made right here in the Mass, because the Mass is the closest thing to heaven on earth. I don't mean that the Mass is close to what heaven is like in the sense that the thrill we get from Mass is like the happiness of heaven—often we don't get any thrill at all. I mean that since Jesus has rightly compared heaven to a banquet, the Mass as a spiritual banquet is intended to be a preview of heaven. The Mass is the celebration of God's family, like our own family dinner at Thanksgiving or Christmas.

Family Dinner

Frequently grandparents have the Thanksgiving or Christmas dinner in their home. They invite their own adult children together with all their grandchildren. Often there are so many people that it is bedlam, but it is really great to get a chance to talk to each other, and of course the grandparents especially want to have a word with everyone who comes. Usually everybody brings something for the meal; one will bring the salad and another the dessert and so on. It's a practical thing, with so many mouths to feed, but it is also a way of showing love and respect for the grandparents, for the food is really a form of gift. Then the climax of the celebration comes when everyone sits down at the table to share the fine dinner.

God's Family

In the Mass God our Father calls us together in his home,

the Church. Here he wants to speak to us, and he does so in the scriptures and the homily. He also wants us to speak to him, and we do so in the prayers and hymns. We even bring some of the food that will be used in the dinner, as the procession with the bread and wine to the altar symbolizes. But that is more than a practical thing because we want to give a gift to God to show our love and respect. The gift we give, however, is not bread and wine, but bread and wine changed into the body and blood of Christ as a sign of his great love on the cross, the kind of love we want to have for God. Then in the climax of our celebration God calls us to his banquet table where we all share in the spiritual food of holy communion.

Heaven

Heaven is God's eternal home, where he wants to have a great big family celebration, an everlasting banquet of joy and happiness. We have been invited. And through all the cares and distractions of this life, and even with a bird in the hand, the way in which we celebrate Mass together with faith and devotion is a sign that we accept the invitation.

C.E.M.

... and to God

During his public life Jesus was recognized as a moral teacher, and so it was not surprising that he was consulted on the matter of whether Jews should pay taxes to a foreign power. Were the Jews by acknowledging the dominance of a foreign government denying God who alone was ruler of Israel? The question could have been a case of conscience for many God-fearing Jews.

Insincere

Those who posed the problem to Jesus, however, were not sincere. They did not hope that he would solve the problem to everyone's satisfaction; rather they wanted to trick Jesus by means of a dilemma so that they could be rid of him. A simple reply that the tax should be paid would have made him look like a traitor to God. A simple denial would have left him open to the danger of being denounced to the Romans as a seditionist. But Jesus refused to be trapped. When he asked to see the coin used for the tax, one of his adversaries produced, of course, a Roman coin. The possession and use of the Roman coin was itself a sign that the Jews had submitted to Roman authority. Actually it was at the invitation of the Jews that the Romans first entered Palestine as a protectorate when the land was in a state of bloody anarchy. The people had received and continued to receive benefit from Roman rule, and as a result had assumed obligations as well. Moreover, some in the crowd surely should have remembered that God had previously used foreign rulers to guide the destiny of his people without any abdication of his own kingship over them. For example, today's first lesson spoke approvingly of Cyrus, who was king of Persia. Cyrus had conquered Babylon and liberated the Jews. He allowed them to return to their native land but continued to exercise authority over them.

More Than Bargained For

So the answer of Jesus, as the questioners stared at the Roman coin, was no evasion of the issue. It clearly implied that it was not only lawful to pay the tax but also of obligation in conscience. "Give to Caesar what is Caesar's," Jesus said. Then he added another admonition, one his questioners had not bargained for: "Give to God what is God's." The gospel goes on to say that they were "taken aback by this reply." After all, they thought, who had to tell them to give to God what was God's? Jesus' statement insinuated that they had asked the wrong question and that they were remiss in their religious duties. Considering the insincerity of the questioners as well as their smugness in matters religious, it is not unlikely that such an insinuation was precisely what Jesus intended by his unexpected remark.

Freely Given

As a matter of fact the Jews were going to pay the tax, no matter what they thought about its propriety. The Romans would see to that, by force if necessary. But God asks only for a service that is freely given. If that service does not spring freely from religious convictions, then in God's eyes it is worthless, and he doesn't want it. God forces no one to be religious. The questioners, then, needed to be reminded that a legalistic approach to religion and a merely external observance of the law were hardly ways of giving God what is his.

Application

Does this gospel have an application today? Well, you can

look at any coin in your pocket or purse and see that the inscription on the back says "United States of America." Since we enjoy benefits from our government, we owe taxes. Perhaps, however, you would like to know whether taxes are excessive, and whether excessive taxes must be paid. Or it may be that you do not approve of how your tax dollars are spent, and you want to know whether taxes must be paid in that case. But then you are getting into a matter of personal opinion, aren't you? I am sure that you do not want me or any priest to stand in the pulpit and give you what is solely a matter of personal opinion. Besides, whether you think taxes are just or not, whether you approve of the way the government is using the money or not, you will still have to pay taxes. The Internal Revenue Service will see to that, as well as the merchant who simply will not sell you something without collecting the sales tax.

Give to God

Very frankly the point we all need to be concerned with is that we must give to God what is God's. And what does that mean? If you tune in at this same time next week you will hear the answer in the gospel. As they usually do on TV, I will give you a preview. Next week you will hear Jesus say, "You shall love the Lord your God with your whole heart, and with your whole soul, and with all your mind." To put it another way, *everything* belongs to God: our bodies, our souls, our talents, even our possessions. It takes a life-long, constant effort to give to God what is his, and it is a supreme obligation in conscience of which we must be frequently reminded. God will not force us to give him his due, for he wants a loving service that is freely given from the conviction of faith.

Today in faith we come before God to offer ourselves completely to him in union with Jesus on the altar. At the conclusion of the Eucharistic Prayer we will profess that all honor and glory belong to God through, with, and in Christ. Fix firmly in your minds the words of that profession: all honor and glory belong to God. Try to live according to those words during this coming week as you make the conscious effort to give to God what is God's—in a word, everything.

C.E.M.

With Your Whole Heart

I think we all recognize that the love we have for a person can find its best expression in time of crisis. A husband may tend to grow thoughtless of his wife and fail to show signs of tenderness and affection, but just let her go into the hospital for a serious operation and he will show how deep his love really is by his worry and concern. Or a mother becomes annoyed with her child who seems always to be complaining, "There's nothing to do around here." After the child is sent out to play he is struck by a car, and in that terrible moment all the love of the mother goes out to her child. It seems a shame that sometimes we wait until a time of crisis to show how great our love is.

No Greater Love

Several years ago a five-year-old girl came down with an extremely rare disease. The doctors understood little about her condition, but they did know that a blood transfusion was imperative, and they wanted her to receive blood exactly like her own, a very rare type. Neither parent had the right type, so the doctors tested the little girl's eight-year-old brother. His type was perfect, but it occurred to the doctor in charge that it would be frightening for a boy of that age to be asked to give blood. The doctor sat the boy down and explained that his sister needed his blood in order to live. The boy's eyes grew bigger and bigger during the explanation, but when the doctor had finished the boy consented and his parents signed the necessary papers. They wheeled the boy into his sister's room and effected the transfusion. When it was all over the little

177

boy looked up at the doctor and asked, "Doctor, when do I die?"

A Shame to Wait

That little boy thought that to give blood to his sister meant that he had to die. How heroic he was! But I am sure that he bickered with his sister and teased her as older brothers do. There were times when he did not want her around as he played with his buddies. But despite all that, he did build within his heart a great love for his sister. In one sense it seems a shame that he waited until a time of crisis to show it.

Love For God

And it is a shame too if we wait until a time of crisis to show our love for God. In our daily lives we can tend to drift away from God, to forget about him, to fail to show the love and tenderness that we should. Sometimes, when God's law gets in the way of what we want to do, we may even wish that he were not around. Today Jesus tells us that we must love God with our whole heart—that means that we must love God all the time, in little things as well as big things. We should not wait until we come face to face with some great problem. Nor can we afford to wait, because we do not know how much love we have built up within ourselves to meet the crisis. Love grows in only one way—by loving.

The Mass

The Mass is the best means we have both for expressing our love of God and for growing in that love. Mass makes us think about God. We hear his words in the scriptures and the homily. If a person is not on your mind, you are not really going to be concerned about him. The Mass is also our way of telling God we love him through the prayers and hymns. A husband and wife can actually increase their love by saying that they love each other. A good husband doesn't need some special occasion to bring home a little gift to his wife. In the Mass we give God the best gift possible, the body and blood of Jesus Christ in sacrifice. We pray that Jesus may make of us an everlasting gift to his Father. That means that our love for God should be so great that we are willing to die for him, as the little boy was willing to die for his sister.

Love also grows from being with the person we love. In holy communion we come into intimate contact with God our Father through the precious body of Jesus Christ, his son.

Participation

Of course the Mass will not automatically help us grow in our love for God, just as human relationships do not grow automatically. People in a family can talk to each other without really communicating. They can physically dwell together under the same roof like boarders without any real personal relationship. They can even eat at the same table without feeling any more sense of intimacy than do people at the same lunch counter in a coffee shop. Growth in love demands effort, especially the effort on your part. You must get involved. God is talking to you and you must listen. When you talk to God, you must mean what you say. The prayers in the leaflet missal and the hymns are cold, dead print on a page. It is up to you to give those words life and meaning. When Jesus renews his sacrifice through the action of the priest, you are not just a spectator. You must actively join with the priest in offering yourself as a victim with Christ. At communion time you must be thinking about the fact that Jesus wants to draw you to himself so that you may share in his own family-like relationship as a child of God the Father.

Not Routine

The Mass should never be just routine. It is too vital to our relationship with God. The real test of our love for God will come on a day of crisis. Meanwhile, let us use the Mass as our means for growing in our love for God, a love so strong that we will be willing to die for him.

C.E.M.

When the Saints Come Speaking Out

A few years ago a French Canadian newspaper reported an incident that happened in Moscow. The Russian State Theater was presenting a comical farce entitled "Christ in a Morning Coat." The purpose was to discredit Christ, the Church, and the Bible. Rostowzew, a comic actor and an avowed Marxist, was the star. He came to the stage and sat down on an altar piled high with vodka bottles. He put on his "morning coat" and began to read the Sermon on the Mount. It seems he was supposed to make it sound funny. But he seriously began to read: "How blest are the poor in spirit: the reign of God is theirs. Blest too are the sorrowing: they shall be consoled. . . ." He paused and the audience was quiet, no longer laughing. Then Rostowzew continued until he finished the entire reading. He piously made the Eastern sign of the Cross at the end, shouted, "Lord remember me in your kingdom," and walked off stage. The stunned audience left the theater rather confused. No other details are known except the play was withdrawn the next day.

Poor Saints

All of us, even a Russian actor, are called to be saints. Some, like the early martyrs, seem to do it with a flourish and influence others. But most of us have to settle with the annoying feeling that we're trying to be good, but are a long way from canonization. We might even yearn for a time when, for our love of Christ, we could accept the sword. At least that would be quick and we'd have something to show for our efforts.

No Challenge?

But I suspect part of the trouble is that we are not being challenged to be saints in a practical way. How moved we are when we meet the mother of six children who tries to spend at least half an hour in prayer each day. We're impressed by the man who always makes a visit to church on his way home from work. We marvel at the person who shares the joy of his Cursillo with everyone. When we hear things like this, a little light dawns. A voice inside says: "You could try the same thing. After all, the kids are in school, or napping; or you pass within a block of church on the way home."

Other men and women like ourselves with just as many things to do and problems on their minds have reached out for Christ and found him. If there were a book on the market: *Guaranteed Way of Seeing Jesus Christ* most of us would read it. We don't lack the desire of being a saint (one in union with Christ). We're just missing someone to help us try, or show us how.

Proposals

Today's feast prompts several proposals. One is to find the lives of some recent saints and look into the ways they discovered Christ. Another is to talk with friends and ask how they've uncovered ways to pray. We all have some friends who are close to sainthood. But most important, speak with Christ himself during this Mass. He is willing to give us his hand to help us come closer. But we have to reach out. We have to give him a few minutes each day. We have to stop once in a while to visit church. And probably hardest, we have to be willing to speak out about Christ. It's amazing how strong our faith can become if we hear ourselves speaking about Christ. To be a saint means to go out on a limb, to share and seek Christ in an open way. The Greek word for martyr means one who gives witness. It might

182

be easier to be a saint if more of our friends spoke about Christ. And what will start them, unless we speak first?

Share the Joy

Statistics for the early 1970's show that the number of converts to the Catholic faith are steadily going down. This is too bad. While the Vatican Council blessedly suggests respect for our brother Christian churches, we're not absolved from following the basic human desire to share a good thing, to show something valuable to others, to give witness to Christ and the Church we love. We might even be so bold as to invite our non-Catholic friends to our Sunday Mass. We would do this simply to show the joy we have found in Christ and in the Church. Non-Catholics have been doing this for years. The point is: if we want to be saints, we have to be willing to brag about our faith. We should be eager to speak of Christ to others.

Ask Christ during this Mass to show himself plainly to you, help you to speak of him to others, and make you a martyr (one who gives witness), a saint. Blest are you who go out of your way to share the joys of knowing Christ and his Church. Be glad and rejoice for your reward in heaven is great.

M.M.R.

One is Your Teacher

A priest once remarked, "I know that it is a shame that I do not practice what I preach, but it would be far worse if I were to preach what I practice." The statement was made in good humor and by a very fine priest who did practice what he preached. And yet it reflects rather well what Jesus is talking about in today's gospel. Jesus does not condemn preaching, only bad example. He does not repudiate authority, only authoritarianism.

Scribes and Pharisees

As a matter of fact we are not inclined to have a very favorable attitude toward anyone who does not practice what he preaches. More seriously, we are not inclined to follow what he has to say. You can imagine how you would feel if your doctor were to insist that you give up tobacco for your health's sake as he blows cigarette smoke in your face. But think about your reaction for a moment. What the doctor is telling you about the danger of smoking is based on pretty solid evidence and research. If you were to reject his advice simply because he is not following it himself, whom would you be harming except yourself?

The scribes and the Pharisees were spiritual doctors, some of whom were not practicing what they preached. In that they were definitely wrong. On the other hand, since they had succeeded Moses as spiritual leaders in Israel, as Jesus pointed out, their teaching should be followed, but not their example. To allow their bad example to obscure the truth of their teaching was only to do harm to oneself.

184

Bishops and Priests

Sometimes you hear about people who have left the Church because they maintain that bishops and priests do not practice what they preach. Even if their claims were true, such people should remember that our Lord himself in today's gospel told the people to follow the teaching of their leaders because they had succeeded Moses, even though they did not follow that teaching themselves. But wait a minute. Who really is the teacher of our faith? Who really is the preacher to whom we must listen? "One is your teacher." It is Jesus Christ. The pope, the bishops, the priests only hand on the word of Christ. Notice that Paul the Apostle commended the people of Thessalonica because they received his preaching, not as the word of men, but as it truly is, the word of God (second reading).

Example of Jesus

The real question, then, centers around the example of Jesus, the Teacher. And he certainly was one who practiced what he preached. Jesus told us to love our enemies, and he redeemed those who by sin were his enemies. He said that we should do good to our persecutors, and he forgave those who put him to death. He proclaimed that no one could have greater love than to lay down his life for a friend, and he died out of love for his Father and us. The very best sermon at any Mass is still the example of Christ, which is made present on our altar: the sacrificial offering of himself to his Father.

Lesson for All

There is a lesson in today's gospel for all of us. Those of us who are ordained ministers must recognize our obligation to practice what we preach. You are right in reminding us of our failures to do so. Moreover we must remember what Jesus said

185

about avoiding titles, such as rabbi, teacher, or father. These titles were applied at various times to Jesus himself, who never rejected them, and of course there was nothing wrong in them. What makes them wrong for us is taking them seriously as titles of personal excellence as if Jesus were not the true teacher in the Church, or as if the purpose of priestly fatherhood were not to draw people only to God the Father in heaven, and not to ourselves. Jesus does not condemn authority, for he gives it to his ministers. But he does condemn authoritarianism, the attitude that authority is a personal characteristic to be used without regard for the teaching of Christ and without reliance on his grace.

There is also a lesson for you who have been baptized into the faith. You must heed the word of God, no matter who the preacher may be. And you too must give good example by practicing that preaching. Frankly the best stimulus I have to be a better priest is the faith and devotion I see in the people I serve. You also owe mutual support to each other. It is a sad, discouraging experience for a person to find that he stands almost alone in his practice of the faith among those with whom he lives and works and prays. Moreover, studies have shown that the rate of converts is off. What will bring others to Christ is your own good example in all the circumstances of your life.

Practice

I hope and pray that no one will ever have to say of any priest, "It is a shame that he does not practice what he preaches, but it would be far worse if he were to preach what he practices." I also hope and pray that all of you will always receive the Christian message, not as the word of men, but as it truly is, the word of God, for one is your Teacher, Jesus Christ.

C.E.M.

Heaven, Not Hollywood

The master of surprise is probably Alfred Hitchcock. Movie-goers are glued to their seats waiting for the bizarre element that throws everything into chaos. But movies seldom are real life. Most of us follow the familiar bit of wisdom, "Always be ready for the unexpected." Everyone from automobile safety councils to the Boy Scouts suggest preparedness. Have plenty of "Oh-Boy-Frozen-Delites" on hand for the last minute company.

Jewish Wedding

Yet in spite of all the warnings, we occasionally wind up being caught off-guard. So it isn't unusual in all the planning for a big wedding feast, as we have in the gospel, that some discovered late in the evening that they were running low on torch fuel. Jewish wedding celebrations were all-night affairs. And the local customs suggested that the groom had to "collect" his bride at her family's home and then bring her to his home. Meanwhile the guests went to the groom's home to prepare for the dusk-til-dawn party. Once everyone arrived, the doors and windows were bolted down and barred for the night. The process involved in opening up was so awkward and troublesome that no one in their right mind ever expected the doors to be opened at night.

Problem

Taking all this into consideration, the situation of the slow-bridesmaids-being-locked-out isn't a problem. But the attitude of the groom is. The groom represents Christ. And the banquet

187

is heaven. His reaction is hardly filled with "Christian" pity. To bar the careless from a banquet is a small thing. To bar them from a joyful eternity is something serious.

But evidently Christ intends the lesson to be painfully clear. When it is a matter of the Second Coming and entrance into the heavenly kingdom, the criterion won't be pity, but justice. We either have what it takes, or we can't come in. So often we're tempted to say there couldn't be a hell. God wouldn't be that mean. But the simple fact is that God the Father doesn't and won't, choose hell for us. We have to do this for ourselves. Anyone who goes to hell isn't forced. He has to buy his own ticket, get on the train, and go. You have to want to go to hell to get there.

Brighter Side

But St. Paul suggests we look at the brighter side. God the Father intends that Jesus bring with him those believing in him. And for those who are friends of Christ, the Second Coming will be a joyful banquet. St. Paul was looking beyond cinema-scope and stereo sound when he suggested "eyes have not seen, nor ears heard what God has in store for us." Nor do we have to fear if we're the good ones or the "bad guys." It's not too hard to tell those who are earnestly trying to be good Christians from those not bothering to try.

Be Careful

But we do have to be careful. The Lord is still the Director and Producer of our lives. He'll decide when our life-movie is to end. It might be an abrupt ending which no one in the "audience" was expecting. Keep your eyes open for you know not the day or the hour. Even make a few preparations now, to avoid being caught short. Try a little extra penance and prayer.

Real Message

The moral is: don't be so confident and lighthearted about heaven that you sit down on the job and stop working. St. Paul warned the early Christians against this. But don't be afraid of hell either. A person who is reasonably trying to be good, lovingly receiving Christ each Sunday, can be confident about heaven, like the child who deep down knows he is loved and wanted by his parents, in spite of the occasional threats of the "wood shed."

The outcome of the last reel of our lives shouldn't be a mystery. Nor should we fear a Hitchcock surprise ending. If we're good Christians we can be certain that at the Second Coming the Lord himself will come down to meet us and we shall be with the Lord unceasingly. Console one another with this message.

M.M.R.

Purpose and Value

Jesus found it necessary to tell the parable you have just heard because as human beings we often fail to use our God-given talents. There are no doubt many reasons why we so fail, but I am convinced that one of the greatest obstacles to progress in our lives is not a lack of opportunity, or inability, or even laziness. It is boredom. Boredom is cold water on the fire of enthusiasm and enterprise. But why are we bored? We get up in the morning and go to bed at night, and in between it is just the same thing over and over again. Is repetition the reason for our boredom? I really don't think it is quite that simple. Actually we can do routine things without finding them monotonous provided we see purpose and value in them. Boredom comes with repetition only when repetition seems pointless.

Continued Creation

Think for a moment about God in his act of creation, as he brought something out of nothing; as he made the universe from a void, as he produced life from stillness. Now there is work with a purpose. If we may speak humanly of God, what a thrill creation must have been for him, what a feeling of accomplishment! But in one sense his work of creation is still going on, and God wills to give each of us a share in continued creation through our human work. God could have made this world to operate like some kind of massive computer without any human involvement, but he didn't want to do it that way. God has put the world and all its marvelous resources into our human hands. He entrusts to us the responsibility of actualizing its potential. Exalted though that may sound, and is, it includes

190

not only the stunning accomplishments of modern science, but all the ordinary chores of every day life as well. It means earning a living and doing housework, going to PTA meetings and Pop Warner football games, repairing your car and washing the dishes.

Purpose

Listen to this official teaching of the Church in the words of the Second Vatican Council: "While providing the substance of life for themselves and their families, men and women are performing their activities in a way which appropriately benefits society. *They can justly consider that by their labor they are unfolding the Creator's work" (The Church in the Modern World,* 34.). This teaching should give a sense of purpose to all that we do, however simple, for human work is truly a sharing in the thrilling act of God's creation itself.

Value

But there is more. Human work not only has a supreme purpose. It is also holy with a great spiritual value. Jesus gave it that value when he became a human being like us. Listen again to these important words of the Second Vatican Council: "By his incarnation the Son of God has united himself in some fashion with every man. He worked with human hands, he thought with a human mind, acted by human choice, and loved with a human heart. He blazed a trail, and if we follow it, life and death are made holy and take on a new meaning" *(The Church in the Modern World,* 22.). Yes, if we only follow the trail blazed by Jesus, everything will take on a new meaning. If we could only keep firmly in mind that human activity has purpose and value, then even the most ordinary, routine matters should not be boring. We should approach them with the enthusiasm of God in his act of creation and with the zeal of Jesus in his human life.

The Mass

Our celebration of Mass is a constant reminder of the meaning and value of our lives. In the Mass God takes the most ordinary things possible, bread and wine, made food and drink by the work of human hands, and gives them a whole new meaning and value as they are changed into the body and blood of Christ. Their new meaning is that as a gift to God they become an act of worship. Their new value is that they are the most precious gift possible. What could be more precious than the body and blood of Jesus Christ! But the Mass is more than a reminder, for God invites us to offer our lives too as a gift to him. In the Mass our gift becomes one with that of Christ, and thereby takes on a special meaning and a precious value, far above that of simple human activity. Our offering should include everything: our joy and our sorrow, our successes and our failures, our pains and our pleasures—and, oh yes, our feelings of boredom too. Our celebration of Mass should make Sunday the brightest day of the week.

No Blue Monday

Of course tomorrow will be Monday again as we return to our weekly routine, but it need not be a blue Monday. Monday and all the other days of the week can each be a Sun-day if we illumine them with the brightness of their true meaning and value in God's plan. Let's try it! Let's try to take from this Mass a sense of the worth of human activity. Then we have a chance of overcoming the obstacle of boredom, and we will have the hope of hearing from Jesus when he comes in judgment: "Well done! You were dependable in small matters. Come, share your master's joy!"

C.E.M.

192

Stewards of Christ the King

On November 22, 1963, the people of the United States and indeed of almost the whole world were shocked at the news that President John Kennedy had been shot to death. For four days, from the day of the assassination until the day of burial, most Americans sat stunned before their television sets as the aftermath of the terrible tragedy was revealed before their eyes. At the time some people asked the question, "How could God, who rules the world, allow such an evil thing to happen?"

End of the World

It is certainly true that God the Father has absolute power and control over his creation. It is also true, as we will hear in the preface today, that the Father has anointed Jesus Christ, his son, as universal king. Today's feast, however, brings out the fact that Jesus has chosen to exercise the fullness of his kingship only at the end of the world when he will come again in all his glory. That is one reason why we celebrate this feast of Christ the King on the last Sunday of the liturgical year.

Trust

Meanwhile Jesus has put the world into our hands in trust. We are stewards of the king. A steward does not have dominion over his master's goods; he cannot do whatever he wants with them. He must use them carefully and prudently as his master wishes. In other words, what we have does not belong to us in any absolute way. This is not the doctrine of communism,

193

which denies the right to private property. Such a denial is not in accord with Christian teaching. On the other hand, the man who says, "I earned it; it's mine and I can do with it whatever I want," does not know whereof he speaks. This world with all of its resources belongs to God. Without those resources we could never survive. Moreover, it is God who has given us the intelligence we use in developing the goods of this world. It is God who gave us the strength we use in earning a living. So whatever we have, even though it was acquired at the expense of our arms and in the sweat of our brows, belongs really to God. He has entrusted these things to us until Christ comes in glory at the end of time to claim his kingdom.

Accounting

When Christ does come at the end of time he will demand an accounting of our stewardship. He will want to know whether we have used his goods carefully and prudently. He will want to know whether we have been selfish and greedy, or loving and generous. Actually, however, Christ will not wait until then to check up on us. Frankly, you might even say that he is just a little sneaky about checking up on us all the time. You see, he is not confined to heaven. He is still walking this earth in our fellow human beings. In a special way he is present in the poor and the needy, and in and through them he will know how we are using the things he has entrusted to us.

Recall the gospel you heard proclaimed a few minutes ago. Jesus declared that when he comes in glory, he will judge us on how we have treated him as he is found in his brothers. How mysterious are his words: "I assure you, as often as you did it for one of my least brothers, you did it for me." Mysterious words, yes, but true. There is no reason to water down this truth: Jesus somehow is really present in our fellow human beings, even in those in whom we might least expect to find him.

194

A Further Implication

When you think about it, those in need have even some kind of a right to be helped by us. I don't mean a right in strict justice, as a man has a right to a day's pay for a day's work. It is a right without a special name. It is a right based on the fact that Jesus lives within others, especially the needy. And remember, whatever we have, we hold in trust as stewards; it all belongs to Jesus. When he asks us for help in his poor, he is only asking for what belongs to him. We have to stop thinking exclusively of our own rights. We must soberly listen to the words of Jesus: "I was hungry and you gave me no food. I was thirsty and you gave me no drink. I was away from home and you gave me no welcome, naked and you gave me no clothing. I was ill and in prison and you did not come to comfort me." We must not dare to protest: "Lord, when did we see *you* in such need and neglect you," because if we do, he will answer, "I assure you, as often as you neglected to do it to one of these least ones, you neglected to do it to me."

Don't Look Up

When President Kennedy was shot, some people looked up to heaven and asked, "How could God allow such an evil thing?" Maybe we at times, disturbed and uncomfortable about the poverty and need in our own country, have asked: "How can God allow such an evil?" Both questions are wrong. We should not look up to heaven to God. We should look at ourselves and ask, "How can we allow evil? Why have we not overcome hatred with love? Why have we not overcome poverty with generosity?"

No Anxiety

On this feast of Christ the King, we must recognize that

we share in Christ's kingly power, that he has entrusted us with his earthly kingdom until he comes in judgment. We must pray that we will live in accord with the truth we proclaim to Christ: "The kingdom, the power, and the glory are yours, now and forever." Then we will indeed be protected from "all anxiety as we wait in joyful hope for the coming of our Savior, Jesus Christ."

C.E.M.